Even God Can Be Fooled

*I*t was obvious even to an unbeliever that God was, for some reason, angry at Mollie Rivka Sennowitz. Why this was so was impossible to understand. She was such a good woman. She kept the laws of Judaism, she shared what little she had with those who had less and yet it seemed that she was cursed.

As a young woman in Russia around 1890 she knew that her prospects in life were not bright. She was small, with wispy light brown hair. When she walked it was with a pronounced limp. She was no beauty and her family had no money for a dowry. Certainly she wasn't a bargain on the marriage market in the small shtetl in Russia where she grew up. Yet the catch of the town, the brightest scholar, fell in love with her and against all tradition married his love rather than the bride his parents had chosen for him.

At first everything seemed to be perfect. They were very much in love, his studies were earning him a place of respect in the community and they were blessed with two little boys, Moshe and Aaron. My grandmother, for that was who Mollie Rivka came to be, stayed home and cared for the house and the children while her husband studied the holy books.

He came home one day and told her in a very excited voice that he was going to spend a few months in a neighboring town at the yeshiva of a very prestigious rebbe. It would mean a separation but it was a great honor and a once in a lifetime opportunity. "We will be lonely," he told her. "But God must have ordained this and so it will be good." They had no wealthy sponsor to push him ahead. He had gotten this chance purely on his scholarship. He could not have refused to go.

What started with high hopes finished in tragedy. He was brought home a few weeks later with a raging fever. Mollie Rivka nursed him as best she could but he died within three days of his homecoming. As if that were not enough, both boys caught the disease, whatever it was and within a week they died as well. She was alone, a poor widow with no one to support her. What kept her going was her determination that she must go on.

Then Julius Sennowitz came into her life. My grandfather was a romantic, something of a blowhard. The father of a daughter. (By a previous marriage? Illegitimate? We never knew. Those kind of things were not spoken about.) He was as poor as she was. They married and had a child who died in infancy. The following year my Uncle Charlie was born. They thanked God that he was healthy. Well, she thanked God; Grandpa was a socialist and had no time for deities.

Julius, who could not eke out a living in Russia, announced that he was going to take his wife and son to America, to a land where there were no pogroms and people could live in dignity, even get rich.

They booked passage on a ship which my Bubba told us was called the "Retze". As a child I remember hearing how awful it was in steerage. My grandmother was pregnant again, the sea was rough and the trip took three weeks. It must have been hell. But finally the day came when they passed the Statue Of Liberty and arrived in the "Goldene Medina." Years later we found out the real name of the ship was the "Red Sea".

The "Amerikaner" baby was born and named Yankel. Grandpa somehow managed to accumulate enough money to buy a kosher chicken market in Brownsville, Brooklyn where Grandma—after having seen to the two boys, cleaned the house and washed the clothes—would then go and wait on the customers.

A kosher chicken market differed markedly from the kind of shops we know today. It was full of cages crammed with cackling fowl. The customers would come in, pass the time of day with Grandma, and then pick the chicken which they wanted to broil or roast for dinner. If soup or stew was to be the end product, a much older and tougher bird would be required. All this necessitated a great deal of discussion which took place in Yiddish accompanied by broad gestures.

Finally, when the negotiations were completed, Grandma would take the selected bird, tuck it under her arm and slit its throat. She would hold it head-down so that the blood would run onto a drain in the floor. Though this maneuver guaranteed that the chicken was kosher, the bird did not submit quietly. The whole procedure was accompanied by squawks and violent flapping of wings. (I watched it once at age six and wouldn't go near a bird of any kind for years.) After the bird quieted down Grandma would eviscerate and pluck it.

She did this day-in and day-out, though most of the time she was either pregnant or nursing. Grandpa wasn't much help. He was too busy solving the problems of the world to pay attention to mundane matters such as supporting a family and running a business. So, while she worked, he attended meetings to discuss the future of the working man.

Now she was pregnant again. How she wished that she could have a girl. She knew that one did not question what God sent but if she could choose....She kept her wishes to herself and went on with her work.

This story was told and retold in our family. Grandma was in her ninth month. She was large and found it hard to move around on her lame legs. As usual she was in the market when one of her customers came in. To hear her describe it the woman was rich and spoiled. I'm not sure what Grandma's definition of rich was although I am sure that it differed greatly from mine. At any rate, the woman came in, sat down on a chair and said to Grandma, "Mollie Rivka, get me a glass of water please. I'm exhausted. I'm three months pregnant you know." Obediently, Grandma did as she was asked. One didn't question a customer.

That afternoon Grandma went into labor and my mother was born. It should have been a moment of great joy but while she was delivering the baby, Yankel, aged two, got hold of the button hook my grandfather used to button his shoes and took out his eye. By the end of the week he had died of the resultant infection. Again my grandmother had to face the loss of a child.

In the course of the next six years my mother grew into a sweet and pretty child with the sunny disposition she maintained all her life. Her little brother Sammy was born and the life of the Sennowitz family seemed to settle into a routine. Grandpa studied and lobbied for the socialist system which would erase poverty from the world while Grandma did her bit to erase poverty from her family.

But the problems of the family were far from over. My mother awoke one morning with a high fever. Grandma did not need a thermometer to tell her that this was a very sick child. She put her lips to her child's head and knew at once that this was serious and in spite of the expense they called the doctor. He looked at the frightened parents and said,"Pneumonia. You'll have to wait for the crisis. Then we will know if she will pull through. It is God's hands. Pray for his mercy."

God's hands! They had had enough of God's mercy. Were they going to lose this precious girl as they had their four sons? They must do something and do it right away.

Next door to them lived a family by the name of Davis. Mrs. Davis had given birth to thirteen children and thirteen were still alive. Any sensible person could see that God liked the Davis family and extended His protection to them. Their plan of action was simplicity itself. All that was needed was to make God think that little Minnie was a Davis and not a Sennowitz and she would be on the road to complete recovery.

They bundled the feverish child up as warmly as they could and Grandpa and Mr. Davis took her to the shul. Grandpa gave Mr. Davis eighteen pieces of silver, eighteen being the numerical equivalent for "Chai", the Hebrew word for life. The rabbi said a prayer and inscribed Minnie Sennowitz in whatever kind of holy book he used for this kind of thing. (The fine details of the transaction were never explained to me.) She officially became Minnie Davis. Then she was taken back home to her mother. We sophisticated moderns may laugh at this kind of primitive superstition but it worked. Within a few days Minnie was weak but recovering.

Years later when my father went to ask for my mother's hand in marriage he was told that he had to go and "buy her back from old man Davis."

A Debt Repaid

My father was sixteen when the "shipstickets" came from his father and older brother. As the family hastily packed their few belongings my father turned to his mother and said, "Mamma, you said I could have a new pair of shoes. The ones I have are too small for me."

"Sinai, we have no money. Papa and Louis sent just enough for the tickets. The shoes will fit Joe. Give them to him. We'll have to think of something to do for you."

My father thought that all of this was fine for his younger brother, Joe, but what about him? It left him without anything on his feet for a November crossing of the Atlantic. What could they do? It seemed like a hopeless situation until a neighbor by the name of Label Friedman, hearing of the problem, made an offer.

"I haven't any extra shoes," he said "but I do have a pair of old rubbers you could have. They're not in very good shape, but they are better than nothing and you need them worse than I do."

"How will I ever be able to repay you?" Dad asked. "We'll be so far away and probably never see one another again."

Label smiled. "Who knows what the future will hold? Maybe one day you will return the favor. Take the rubbers and good luck to you."

His generosity was gratefully accepted and the family, Dad sporting his rubbers, left for America, sure that they had seen the last of Label Friedman.

Years went by and my father became a successful merchant. He owned a chain of men's clothing stores called Howard Clothes and decided to open a store in Philadelphia where his older sister Lena lived. He stopped to see her before he went to look at store locations, and she said to him, "Sinai, do you remember Label Friedman who gave you the rubbers back in Russia? Well, he's here in Philadelphia."

"What does he do?"

"He's a banana peddler."

"Can you find out where he lives?" asked my father.

"Of course. He, his wife, Sara, and their six children live in a basement apartment on Elm Street. It's only a few minutes from here."

Dad asked the real estate agent who was to show him property in Philadelphia if he would mind stopping at Elm Street for a few moments. There Dad and Label had an emotional reunion.

My father asked, "How is life treating you, Label?"

"I can't complain," he answered. "Of course it gets a little cold pushing this cart in the winter and the bananas freeze and turn black. In the summer a lot of them rot from the heat. But we have enough to eat and at least I know that my children will have a better life."

"Let's see if I can help you," my father said.

Getting back in the car, my father told the real estate agent, "Now I not only need a store for Howard Clothes but I also need a store for my old friend so he can sell his wares without catching pneumonia. When you find it I'll pay the first two years rent. After that we'll see if he can manage for himself."

I must admit that I had never heard this story until the day of my father's funeral. Dad died on November 11, 1957 and the funeral was held at Temple Rodolph Sholom since the regular funeral parlor was too small for the huge crowd which gathered to pay tribute to that good man. As my mother led us down the aisle of the crowded sanctuary, she said, "Girls, hold your heads up high. You have a lot to be proud of." And we certainly did.

The Rabbi must have spoken about Dad's generosity and kindness, but he didn't make any impression on me. I can't even remember who he was. It was what happened after the ceremony that I'll never forget.

Mom, my three sisters, and I were in the lead car in the funeral cortege. We were parked on the corner of 81st Street and Columbus Avenue waiting for the cars to assemble when a man came running down the street shouting, "Mrs. Kappel! Mrs. Kappel!" He had a heavy Yiddish accent and it came out sounding like,"Mrs. Koppelye! Mrs. Koppelye!"

Mom got out of the car and the man threw his arms around her. "Oy! Oy!" he said. "What have I done? This man bought me a store. He took me off the street. He did everything for me and I came too late to his funeral." The words and the sobs came pouring out of him. "I missed the early train from Philadelphia and had to take the next one. He would never forgive me and I'll never forgive myself."

"Label, Label," my mother said, "he would understand. People miss trains."

She finally got him under control and came back into the car to explain to her very curious daughters who this man Label Friedman was, since none of us had ever heard of him or of this particular story of kindness reciprocated. Sad as we were we started to laugh, knowing that to my father, coming late to anything was a cardinal sin. We wondered if he would have forgiven poor Label. Perhaps in his case he would have made an exception. Although I wouldn't bet on it.

was ground, kneaded into bread and baked. Finally it was served to us with Pepsi Cola! I shuddered at the thought of how unsanitary it all must be, but of course I ate and thanked everyone profusely.

Next day we went to a well-baby clinic run by the Joint. The infant mortality rate at that time was astronomical but most of the deaths were preventable with proper nutrition and sanitation. Pregnant woman were urged to come to the clinic every day for food supplements. After their babies were born they returned for medical examinations, powdered milk and a daily bath for the child. Any mother who kept up the visits for at least three months was entitled to keep the small red plastic tub in which her child had been bathed. The promise of such a treasure as well as the joy of seeing her child live, kept most of them coming back. The death rate dropped dramatically. Once that happened it became even more vital to get them to Israel as there really was no chance for most of them to make a decent living in Morocco.

As I have said, there were the three T's, tinea, trachoma and tuberculosis. The people of the Joint were busy shaving the heads of children with tinea (ring worm of the scalp) and giving the parents soap and disinfectant to help to keep their heads clean. At the same time they were medicating and feeding those with tuberculosis. As for the trachoma, about a dollar's worth of Penicillin, rubbed onto the eye three times a day could cure it. It could not restore sight but it could prevent further blindness.

It was soon discovered that giving the families Penicillin and the instructions just didn't work. They would forget to apply it, misplace it and in some cases, even eat it. Some other way had to be devised so the nurses of the Joint divided the Jewish quarter into districts. They would start at one end of each street, applying the medication as they went. By the time they each had covered one area it was time to go back and start again. After a very few months, trachoma was just a bad memory.

Of course there were also smallpox vaccinations to be given. This the nurses of the Joint did as well. To me they were saintly people.

The trip changed all of my perceptions. When we landed at Idlewild Airport we were met by our eight-year-old son who greeted us with, "Hello Mommy and Daddy. I need an English bike. All my friends have one." Before the trip I might have run out and gotten him one. Now the word "need" had totally different connotations for me. A new bike which cost about eighty-five dollars in those days, could prevent blindness in eighty-five children. I reminded Peter that his three speed bike was only one year old and suggested that he could wait.

Having seen what I had just seen put our lives in a new perspective My purpose was now to raise money to help the wonderful work of the Joint continue. I have spent many years doing just that and loved the feeling that I was able to make a difference in the lives of people I will never see.

Golda and I share a joke

Introducing Moshe Dayan in Jerusalem

With Shimon Peres at the Knesset in Jerusalem

Greeting Ben Gurion

With my idol Eleanor Roosevelt in 1957

Mom and Dad on the beach at Lido in 1928

Mom and Dad in 1919

With my Dad in 1925

Me 1929

can't go home looking like that." He was right and I took his advice, but the truth of the matter is that I was too stimulated to do much resting. The first morning at about six, not being able to sleep, I took the book I was reading, something by Senator Fulbright, a Democrat from Arkansas, and went outside to sit and read by the seashore. There was a young American sitting there. He said good morning, looked at my book and said, "Let me introduce myself. I'm a Protestant right wing Republican Congressman from Iowa and I want to know why you're reading that book."

I answered with a smile, "Glad to meet you. I'm a left wing Jewish woman from New York and I like that book." We both smiled and I asked, "What are you doing here?"

"I'm on the Agriculture Committee and I came here to study Israeli methods of cross-breeding cattle. But I stayed to cheer for these folks. They're great people."

"What is it that you admire so much?" I asked.

He looked at me in amazement and said, "They beat the Commies, didn't they?"

Apparently the victory meant different things to different people. To him it meant a setback for the Soviet Union. To me, it meant that Israel was safe, at least for a little while.

How the Druse Children
Got Their School

*I*t was a spring night in 1968 and I was in Jerusalem, having dinner with my friend, Eliezer Shmueli, the director of the Ministry of Education of Israel, and his wife, Geula. Eliezer turned to me and asked, "How about coming with me to the Druse village of Julis. You will find it a fascinating experience." Then he gave me a quick history of these unique people.

"We think they are European in origin," he said, "although no one is quite sure and some even claim that southern Syria is where they come from. At school we learned they settled in Palestine in the thirteenth century. Since the foundation of the State of Israel they have lived on the best of terms with all of us other Israelis. They're wonderful people and are so loyal that, unlike Arab citizens, they serve in the army and in the border patrol."

He told me that their religion, which is an offshoot of Islam, is so secret that only a few members of the community—The Sheik, The Cadi or high priest, and perhaps one or two others—know the basic laws and they interpret these for all the other Drusim. They are mainly an agricultural people. They are monogamous, don't drink alcohol, and are very family oriented. Their hospitality is legendary.

"They'll press you to eat and drink and consider it an insult if you refuse. You'll come home fatter, but you'll enjoy the experience."

It sounded like a real adventure and I said that I'd be delighted to go. I thought that it was to be a purely social visit but I should have known that Eliezer, ever interested in educating the children of Israel, had a hidden agenda.

During the previous three years I had spearheaded the drive to raise the money to build a school in the city of Dimona, in the Negev. It was one of the first schools built by the Israel Education Fund and because it was such a great success I had developed a reputation of being someone to turn to when a new school was needed. It seemed that the Drusim needed a school, but I had no idea of that when I met Eliezer at eight A.M. in front of the King David Hotel for our drive up to the Galilee.

The Galilee, which is beautiful at any time of the year, was especially lovely with the trees and flowers just coming into bloom. The trip took about two hours, during which Eliezer told me more about the Druse people, for whom he had great admiration. He described their respect for their wives and their pride in their children. "Kemal is a real character," he told me, referring to the Sheik who we were going to visit. "You two should really get along."

Finally we reached Julis, a small village perched on the top of a hill. We began the circuitous route up the hill to the home of Kemal Tarif. As we did, we passed many small clay-colored houses, none exactly identical, but all very similar. There was nothing green in sight and in spite of the fact that this was a fairly prosperous village, it could have used the services of a garbage collector. Old bicycle frames and used furniture littered the dusty streets. We saw a few women who were dressed in long robes, with their faces uncovered. They were surrounded by children. They looked at us with curiosity, waved in a friendly way and went about their business. Apparently outsiders were not a rarity here.

Eliezer stopped the car in front of a two story house which was much larger than any we had passed and which actually had a tree growing in front of it. Later I found out that the house consisted of two identical apartments and that the family lived in the upstairs one in the winter to get the sun's warmth and the downstairs one in the summer in an effort to stay cool. The door was opened by a swarthy man well over six feet tall. He had huge black eyes, a big black mustache and was wearing a long grey robe and a full Arab headdress.

"Welcome to my village and to my home," he said as he ushered us into a large square room. "Please sit down." I looked in vain for chairs and then realized that the walls of the room were lined with upholstered benches. The only other furniture consisted of several small round wooden tables each of which was inlaid with something resembling mother of pearl.

Kemal Tarif, for we had been greeted by the Sheik himself, motioned for us to sit down. After a silence which must have lasted about two minutes, but which seemed like an hour, he turned to me and asked, "How is the health of your mother?"

Since he had never met my mother, I thought it was a rather strange question, but as I had been briefed on Druse etiquette, I replied, "She is well, I thank you, and how is the health of your mother?" His mother was fine as well and, having exhausted that subject, we lapsed back into silence.

A few moments later he turned to me and asked,"May I inquire as to the health of your father?"

I explained that my father had been dead for over ten years and he expressed his condolences. I figured it was better late than never. Now it was my turn.

"And your father, I hope he is well."

Kemal smiled, "Indeed he is and he is hoping to have the honor of meeting you."

I assured him that I was waiting with great anticipation to meet the patriarch of the Druse people. We both smiled. This was hardly the fascinating encounter I had been led to expect, but I was getting into the rhythm of it and beginning to enjoy the minuet.

During the next long pause I took the opportunity to look around. The benches which lined the walls were covered in a mustard-colored silken fabric with turquoise pillows scattered around. On the whitewashed walls were the kind of embroidered pictures which are usually found in souvenir shops. The ones I particularly remember were of the Statue of Liberty and the Eiffel Tower.

At this moment a young woman with black hair, white complexion and very blue eyes entered the room. She wore a long robe and carried a tray. Kemal introduced her to me as his wife who, he proudly explained, was the mother of his four children. She smiled shyly and gestured that I should help myself to the refreshments she had placed on the table in front of me. I looked down and couldn't believe what I saw. The Druse are teetotalers, as I have explained, but, knowing that Americans are not, she had brought me a bottle of Johnnie Walker Black Label Scotch, a shot glass, and a large dish of Jordan almonds. Scotch at ten thirty in the morning! I forgot the warnings about Druse hospitality and said, "Oh, no thank you."

Kemal would not hear of it. "Please, you must drink," he said.

Remembering that I must not offend the Druse sensibilities, I lifted the glass and said "Labriut," (to your health) then drank the Scotch, which I detest at any hour of the day, and drowned out the taste with a few almonds. However that was as much as I could do not to contravene the rules of Druse hospitality. I refused a second drink as politely but as firmly as I could and happily my host didn't press me further.

Kemal gave some sort of signal and his wife reappeared with pots of steaming coffee and small china cups. This is an improvement on the Scotch I thought. Although Kemal's wife waited on us and did not sit down and join in the conversation, he treated her with respect and affection. He never gave her an order, only requests.

"My wife and I would be honored," said Kemal, "if you would meet our children."

"I look forward to that." I really did, this was not just politeness. However, I discovered that I would have to wait for that pleasure. Kemal had another issue on his mind. Having gotten through the preliminaries, he came to what I suddenly realized was the point of the visit.

"Ilana," he said, using my Hebrew name, "we have heard how you were able to build a school for the children of Dimona. We have a serious problem here. We are citizens of Israel and we love our country but because our native language is Arabic, our children go the Arab schools. There they teach them not to love their country, but to hate it. That is not what we want. We want to have our own school and we are sure you can help us to find the money to build it. With the land my family will donate, it would only cost $250,000."

What a bargain! I thought. But all I said was, "I would like nothing more than to see you have your own school, Kemal, but you must understand it is no easy task to raise so much money. I can make no promises."

He took this as an indication of my modesty. He had no doubt of my ability. Of course I could raise the money, he assured me. At this point I was ready to choke Eliezer for having gotten me into this situation.

"I'll try my best," I said, hoping that this was the end of the conversation.

"And you will be successful, Ilana. We have great faith in you."

I changed the subject. "When do I meet your father and your children, Kemal?"

As if by magic, all four children appeared. They must have ranged from about six years to nine months and were fat and cheerful. Their clothes, which were in Arab rather than Israeli style, were brightly colored, well-made and of good material. The three older ones, two boys and a girl, had their mother's blue eyes, while the baby girl's were big and black. All of them were ringed with kohl, a very ancient cosmetic of the Middle East, which, according to Druse tradition, keeps away evil. The kohl, I was told, was applied right after birth and the children wore it until they had passed the danger of childhood disease.

Soon Kemal's father, the Cadi, entered the room. Tarif Tarif (his name is slightly repetitious) was as tall as his son, with a long white beard and a few wisps of white hair showing from under his turban. His bearing was that of a biblical patriarch. The children solemnly kissed his hand.

He bowed to me and said, "It is an honor to have you in my son's home. I can only regret that my wife is in another village visiting friends. On your next trip we must have the honor of your visit in our home."

I promised that I would return soon, after which I went through the same routine as I had with Kemal, about my mother and my father. But, as the Cadi was well into his sixties, I was afraid to ask about the health of his parents, so this conversation was a short one.

Finally we were able to say goodbye and leave. I couldn't wait to get into the car to turn to Eliezer and say, "What did you do to me? It's hard enough to raise money for Jewish schools. Where on earth will I find $250,000 for a Druse school? It wasn't fair to get their hopes up. You've really placed me in a difficult position."

"It was his idea and not mine," said Eliezer. "He read about you and your school in the Jerusalem Post and called and asked me to bring you up."

"Well, it was fascinating, but I'm afraid he won't get his school."

I returned home and completely forgot about the problem of the Druse school. Then one day my secretary came into my office and said to me,"There's a man out here who wants to see you about donating some money."

"Send him in," I said. "I always have time for people who want to give money away."

A dark haired man of about thirty-five or forty came in. He introduced himself and said, "I was told you might help me. My father died a few months ago and left $250,000 in his will. He directed that it go to Israel, but it must be to a program which includes non-Jews. Do you have any ideas?"

Did I have any ideas? I certainly had at least one. I told him about the Druse and he said he thought that was exactly the sort of project his father would have liked. So that is how the Druse children of Julis got their school and I, despite my feeling that I hadn't earned the honor, became an honorary Druse.

Massachusetts, park the car and cross over to the island of Nantucket where he had booked a room at an inn called the Moby Dick which was at the far end of the island. It all sounded salty and romantic to me.

The ferry pulled into the main town of the island and we took a taxi to the Moby Dick. It turned out to be a low white clapboard building which sort of meandered along the beach. Our room was clean and simply furnished, with a double bed and a dresser, totally unremarkable except for one feature: the bathroom locked from the outside. I haven't any idea why it was designed this way but I do remember when Norman, in a fit of playfulness, locked me in. Luckily I was dressed and our room was on the ground floor so I climbed out the window. It sounds adolescent now, but at the time we thought it was hilariously funny.

We took long bicycle rides and wound up lying on the beach, laughing helplessly, trying to get our second wind. As a matter of fact, almost everything struck us as wonderful and funny. We were discovering each other and relishing every moment. We were totally involved with one another. The outside world did not seem to exist.

One morning we came out of the dining room after breakfast and saw a couple standing in front of the building. He was carrying a radio. It had been days since we thought of what the news was, but seeing the radio made us remember that Richard Nixon was deep in the Watergate scandal. As ordinary citizens and as Nixon-haters we were anxious to know what was going on.

We approached them and Norm asked, "Are you going to listen to the nine o'clock news?"

"We sure are," was the reply. "Would you like to join us?"

"Love to," said Norm. "This is Elaine, and I'm Norman Winik." I thought that he had gotten around a delicate situation nicely.

"I'm Doctor Robert Bank and this is my wife June. We're from Allentown, Pennsylvania."

"Allentown!" I said, forgetting that in those days unmarried people traveling together should not play Jewish geography. (Anyway, I didn't think that they were Jewish.) "Perhaps you know my friend, Alex Grass. He lives in Allentown."

"Of course we know him."

Norm was now going to play the game as well. "Do you know Mary Sachs?"

"Certainly do. She's a wonderful woman." Turning to me he continued, "She is so charitable that she does something I'm sure you have never heard of. She borrows money to give to charity."

"I have heard of it," I said, "and I do think it is wonderful to be that caring."

"She borrows money to give to what I consider the most important charity in the world, the United Jewish Appeal."

I usually speak first and think after and this was no exception. "I'm the national chairman of the U.J.A."

"Darling," Dr. Bank called out to his wife, "Mrs. Winik is the national chairman of the U.J.A."

With more self possession than I ever gave myself credit for I said, "Oh, I use the name Siris for that work."

It wasn't easy to listen to the news with straight faces, but somehow we managed. Then we went back to our room and completely fell apart, giggling like ten-year-olds. The national chairman of the U.J.A. traveling with someone to whom she wasn't married! What would the Jewish world think? The Banks would go back to Allentown, spread the word, and my reputation would be down the drain.

We spent the next two days trying to avoid the doctor and his wife. If we saw them coming toward us we turned and went the other way. Finally the day came when we had to leave. We made sure that they did not see us checking out so that there would not be any last minute conversation, and we drew a sigh of relief as we boarded the ferry. No sooner had the ferry pulled away when we heard someone call. "Mr. and Mrs. Winik."

"We've been trying to find you for days," said the ever-cheerful doctor with a smile. "We have very close friends in St. Louis by the name of Mel and Harriet Dubinsky. They are very active in the U.J.A. Do you by any chance know them?"

"Of course I do."

"I knew you would. Tell me again that name you use for the U.J.A. so I can call and tell them that we met you."

As soon as we got home I went into the U.J.A. office to see the executive director, Irving Bernstein. "Irv," I asked, "have you ever had to fire a chairman for moral turpitude? If you haven't, I think you have your first case."

I wasn't fired. What has become commonplace now was beginning to be accepted then. And for some reason, the Banks really believed I was Mrs. Winik and that I used the name Siris for my work. As for our mutual friends, the Dubinskys, they never mentioned anything about it and I never even found out if Dr. and Mrs. Bank ever told them of our meeting.

My daughter, Penny, asked me, "Did you wear a wedding ring?"

"Was I supposed to? I've never done this before, you should have given me some pointers."

nodded emphatically. I had stretched my Yiddish to the limit with my first sentence and so I had to continue in English, but he seemed to understand. "What do you need? We can go to the Friendship Store and buy things for you." The Friendship Store was open only to foreigners who could pay for their purchases in hard currency.

At this moment a Chinese man came running into the room. He smiled at us and said, "I Maxie's friend. I take care Maxie. He need warm blanket and big shirt."

"How about food?" Norman asked.

"I cook for Maxie. I promise his mamma I take care, I do. I make him chicken. He like chicken. I make him Chinese eat, he like that too, but best of all, he like pig." We couldn't resist a smile, the last Jew of China going down eating pork.

We left, found the Friendship Store and bought the blanket, the shirts and lots of canned goods. We brought it all back to Maxie's house, along with a sweater for his friend and a large woolen shawl for the woman whom we had first seen at the window. She thanked us with smiles and gestures and Maxie's friend told us she was Maxie's wife.

I tried to explain to Maxie that I was part of the J.D.C., the people who had been sending him his small stipend for many years. He nodded and I think he understood. By now, we could see he was tiring, so we said goodbye and went back to the group to continue the regular tourist's tour of China.

We never saw Maxie again.

Norm and I returned home and told others about Maxie. He did have a few more Western visitors, but he never left the small room in Shanghai. He died there a few years later. The New York Times ran a story on the obituary pages about the last Jew of China and another chapter of Jewish history was closed.

Naked In The Sinai

The second William Rosenwald Mission (a trip sponsored by a good friend of mine, the great Jewish philanthropist) was going to Israel on November 13, 1981. Norman didn't want to go, but I felt I should, so we decided that he would meet me in Jerusalem on the last day of the mission and we would go on a seven day camping trip in the Sinai. Gene and Emily Grant and Dee Topol, friends of ours also on the mission, were going to join us.

We had researched the available Sinai trips and selected one that was billed as, "In the Footsteps of Moses, Five Days in Sinai by Command Car." We reserved places on that trip, sent our deposits and received instructions to meet in Eilat on a particular day. The itinerary included travel through the desert to Mount Sinai, then all the way down to Ras Muhamed and Sharm El Sheik, which were then in Israeli hands. After all that time in desert terrain we would come back along the coast, stopping at many of the beautiful beaches of the Gulf of Aqaba. We were also told that sleeping bags would be provided but that we should bring sun hats and sunglasses. That was it. We trusted we would find out the rest en route.

The five of us arrived at the Eilat airport after the short flight from Tel Aviv and found three command cars waiting on the tarmac. They were army surplus, with wooden seats and large water tanks strapped to each side. If luxury was what we were looking for, we had come to the wrong place. We looked around at the twenty-five people who were to be our traveling companions and saw that everyone else on the trip was French, young, and part of a Club Mediteranee group. We also realized that although we were in a Jewish country, with the exception of the guides we were the only Jews in sight.

The three handsome young guides greeted us in English and in French and gave us our instructions, which consisted of, "Get on board and drink plenty of water. Your body dehydrates quickly in this heat." That was all.

We did as we were told, the cars started and about thirty bumpy minutes later we came to a halt at a deserted beach.

"O.K. everyone. Let's have a swim!" called Moti, one of the guides.

I was ready. I grabbed my beautiful new Gottex bathing suit and looked around for a place to change. It quickly became obvious to me that there was no such place, so I went behind the command car and wriggled into my suit, making sure that no one was looking. I wondered where everyone else was changing. That problem was soon cleared up. I emerged from behind the truck to see Norm, his mouth hanging open, watching the French women strip off their shirts and shorts and dive in with nothing on but their underpants.

"Why don't you take your top off too, darling?" he asked.

"I can't. It's a one piece suit," I answered with stiff dignity, thinking of the thirty plus years between me and the Gallic bathing beauties. In I went as I was.

The swim was followed by lunch which consisted of open cans of food placed along the sides of the command cars. We all lined up, plastic plates and cutlery in hand and helped ourselves to canned beets, canned asparagus, canned olives, canned peaches, and glasses of tepid water. The girls who had swum topless ate their meals in the same abbreviated outfits. Norm and Gene began to look forward to lunchtime in spite of the quality of the food.

By dinner the air in the desert was cool and so our female fellow travelers put their clothes on. Again we took our plates and helped ourselves from the cans spread along the sides of the cars. Then we all sat down in a large circle around a campfire and toasted one another in warm Israeli wine. It sounds awful, but at the time it seemed perfect. A couple of glasses of wine after a day in the sea and the sun made us both happy and sleepy.

Norm figured out how we could convert our two sleeping bags into one double, so as soon as we had finished dinner we moved away from the group and prepared to bed down for the night. Sleeping under those stars was one of the most incredible experiences I've ever had. I kept waking up to make sure they were real. They were so bright and so close. I watched as they faded and the sun began to rise turning the desert sands a golden pink.

On a more practical note, the guides planted a shovel in the middle of camp with a roll of toilet paper stuck to the top and a package of matches on the sand next to it. One by one we would take the paper, try to find a rock to hide behind, no easy job in the desert, and, having finished, burn the paper. We had to leave the desert as clean as we found it.

After breakfast on the second day we were told we were going to take a walk of about an hour to an oasis where we could swim. We set out, I was again clutching my one piece bathing suit. It must have been one hundred degrees, but the air was so dry that one really didn't feel the heat. Still, the prospect of a swim seemed very inviting.

As we neared the oasis I turned to Norm and said, "The hell with the bathing suit. I'm going to do what everyone else is doing."

"What about Gene Grant?" asked Norm.

"That's his problem," I answered. "When in Rome."

Gene took it very much in stride, although Emily and Dee seemed a little shocked by my decision. As for me, I loved it.

That evening, as we sat around the campfire, Moti came over to me and said, "Ilana, I very much want to know more about the Jews of the United States. How do they feel about Israel? Do they want to come and be part of us? So many things I want to know. Dee said that you would be the one I should talk to. Will you talk to me about it?"

I said that nothing would give me greater pleasure and so every evening Moti and I would discuss the similarities and the differences between our two Jewish communities. Sometimes we talked about the Bible, Jewish philosophers and folk lore.

Our daily program was full. One day we visited a Bedouin camp, where an old man proudly made us mint tea over a brass brazier. On another we got up at three A.M. and climbed Mt. Sinai to see the sun rise from the top. We climbed by way of three thousand steps, the life's work of a Greek monk who lived about two hundred years ago. There were still monks there, holy yes, but dirty as hell. They showed us the skulls of hundreds of monks who had lived and died there, and what they assured us was the original burning bush.

A third day we snorkeled in the clear waters of the Red Sea. We saw what were purported to be the oldest roofed dwellings in the world. Perhaps the ancient Hebrews had built them during their forty years in this desert. One memorable morning we moved our sleeping bag out of the wadi where we had been told not to sleep, just in time to avoid being washed into the sea by a flash flood. Every day was a different adventure, but every evening was basically the same. We would have our cocktail of vodka and warm water, then dinner with warm wine, after which Moti and I would talk.

The trip ended too soon. We said good-bye to our now fully clothed friends and, as we were about to part, Moti came over, kissed me, and said, "Ilana, you can't imagine what an honor it was for us to have had you on this trip. Who would have thought that first day when I saw you swimming naked in the oasis, that you were such an intelligent lady."

I think it he meant it as a compliment. At least I took it as such.

Air Tunisie

*E*veryone has crazy stories about plane trips, how they were bumped from overbooked flights, how they missed a connection because their plane was late, even how the left engine started to smoke half way across the Atlantic. Of course I have had my share, but none of them quite equals our adventure on Air Tunisie.

Norman and I had been in Israel and now, in early October, 1987 we were on our way, first to Tunisia and then to Morocco, to see some Joint Distribution Committee programs in operation. The way to get to Tunis from Tel Aviv was to fly to Cairo, (Egypt having made peace with Israel, transit was now permitted) and after a five hour wait, get an Air Tunisie flight. The idea of five hours in the dirty, run-down Cairo airport didn't please either of us, but the only other option would have been to fly to Paris and change planes there. That would have taken much longer and probably cost twice as much so we decided to make the best of it and go via Cairo.

"It won't be so bad," I said hopefully. "We can always hire a taxi and go into Cairo and spend a couple of hours at the museum."

"Great idea!" said Norman. "Maybe they've improved the lighting since our last trip and we'll be able to see King Tut a little more clearly."

"I doubt it," I answered. "Things move pretty slowly in Egypt. It's only ten years since we were there. That's not a long time in the land of the pyramids. Still, even in the dark mummies can be fascinating."

We passed the time on the short flight encouraging one another. We had just about convinced ourselves we would manage to go into town and have some fun when we landed and were disillusioned. We arrived at the airport and a large Arab in a dirty keffiyah motioned us into a small room. He took our passports, casually threw them into the top drawer of a very dilapidated desk and told us to sit down on one of the wooden benches and wait for our flight. With that he turned and started to leave the room.

"Just a moment, sir," I said, not waiting for Norman to speak, as I could see he was furious at the way we were being treated. Norm is a man who is slow to anger, but the few times I have seen him lose his temper, he really lost it, and I didn't want him to start tangling with the Egyptian authorities, especially with them holding our passports which had many Israeli stamps on them. Perhaps news of the peace treaty hadn't permeated to the airport staff. I continued, "We know that we have five hours to wait. Could you give us back our passports and let us go into Cairo for a cup of tea?" Neither of us drinks tea, but it seemed a ladylike request to make.

He glared at me as though I had insulted his mother and said, "You'll need a visa to get out of the airport and that will cost you four hundred American dollars each."

"Four hundred dollars!" I exclaimed. "Surely there must be some mistake."

"No mistake, lady. You want to go, you give me eight hundred dollars. You don't, I'll let you sit in the main waiting room of the airport. I'll keep your passports and you can come back for them just before your plane leaves."

I looked at Norm who seemed ready to start another Arab-Jewish war and said, "All right, we'll go into the main part of the airport."

"Bastard," muttered Norm, a little too loudly for my taste. "He didn't have to keep the passports. He's just trying to hassle us."

"Well, there's nothing we can do about it. Let's relax. Meanwhile I'll contact Air Tunisie and double-check our reservations."

There was no Air Tunisie desk on the main floor of the airport, but I finally managed to reach them on the telephone. The man who answered was very polite. "Madame," he said in French, "I cannot tell you how sad it makes me that you are not on the manifest for the next flight to Tunis. Perhaps we can get you on the one which leaves tomorrow."

"Don't be ridiculous," I said, mentally thanking my high school French teacher for the fact that I could carry on this conversation without any trouble. "We made these reservations three months ago and I have the tickets with me. Besides, we have people waiting to meet us in Tunis. You must get us on this plane."

"Madame," he said, obviously not too impressed by my argument, "I regret, but there is no room on the plane."

I looked over at Norman who was oblivious to all this, and shuddered to think what his reaction would be to spending the night at the airport. "Where is your office?" I asked.

"We are in the airport on the second floor. However you cannot come up."

"Well, I'm in the main waiting room," I said. "Please come down here, I can't discuss this further on the phone."

"Very well, Madame. I will come down, but it will do you no good." He sounded as if he was losing patience.

A few minutes later I looked up to see a swarthy young man of perhaps thirty-five, dressed in a neat but shabby brown suit. He bowed slightly, told me his name, and showed me the manifest. Our names were not on it. I reasoned, I pleaded and then I threw a small tantrum, shouting at him in a loud voice. "What kind of people are you who don't honor reservations? Can't you see my husband is not well and that we have to be on that plane?" People were beginning to turn and stare at us. The man looked very upset, which is what I had hoped to accomplish.

"All right, Madame," he said, "please do not make a scene. You and your husband are on the flight. See, I am writing your names in right here. We will work it out somehow."

"What are our seat assignments?" I asked.

"There is open seating, Madame. Just get on and take any seat. Adieu, Madame, and a pleasant flight." I'm sure that what he meant was, Go anywhere you want, Madame, only make sure it's far from me. He forced a smile and left.

I turned to Norm who had been watching this whole performance with a mixture of horror and fascination. "Good work," he said, "but I still don't trust him. Let's get our passports and be the first to board the plane."

As soon as the flight was called, we reclaimed our passports, ran to the gate and were the first ones to board. We sat in the second row and watched as the plane filled up. Except for us, the plane carried Tunisians, Moroccans, Egyptians and other Arabs. The sound of variously accented Arabic was everywhere. The crew was about ready to close the doors when an argument broke out. It seems that there were two more passengers than there were seats and the stewardess was having difficulty in explaining to the last two people to board that there was no room for them. The two men were having none of that argument and refused to leave. They had valid tickets. The whole scene was taking place in heated Arabic, but we understood perfectly what was being said. We slouched down in our seats, hoping no one would notice us.

The argument went on and on. The pilot got involved and so did some of the other passengers. The take off was delayed. Finally a Solomonic decision was made. One man was seated in the bathroom, the other one was put in the cockpit. The plane doors closed and we took off for Tunis.

We were greeted by the J.D.C. representative at the Tunis airport. On our way to the hotel she pointed out the sights of the city. We really didn't care, we were on land and safe. Now all would be well. We finally arrived at the Tunis Hilton to hear her say, "There, just across the street, is the world headquarters of the P.L.O." And all our insecurities returned.

The Magic Spell

Masada always works a kind of magic. Standing on top of what was the last home of the Jewish holdouts in the war against the Romans in 73 A.D., I always feel I can see the enemy preparing to besiege the stronghold. In late October, 1980 I led a group of New Yorkers to Masada, many of them for their first visit. The Israeli government allowed us to stay after sunset (Masada usually closes just before it gets dark) so that we could have the great fortress all to ourselves.

My daughter Margot and her two sons, Sam, nine, and Ben, five, were with us. My son-in-law Kenny was spending his sabbatical year teaching at the Technion and Margot had taken a leave from her job so she and the boys could be with him. Of course I asked them to join us.

Sam and Ben became the group mascots. Sam and Margot spoke Hebrew, which impressed the Americans who tend to be notoriously monolingual. Everyone was interested in what it was like to live in Israel, as opposed to coming there on a whirlwind tour, and Margot was kept busy describing the daily life of an Israeli.

For me it was a wonderful chance to do my work and be with my family at the same time, especially since Margot and her family live in Oregon and we don't get to spend nearly enough time together.

We climbed Masada in the early afternoon. Well, some of us climbed, the others took the cable car. Once on the top, we looked around that fascinating and haunted place. Here Eliezer Ben Yair and his people decided it would be better to die than to submit to Roman rule.

Since Masada was built as a residence for Herod, it contained all of the conveniences of the world of that day. Only ruins remain but there are enough of those so we could sense what life must have been like in ancient times. There was the terrarium and the calderium, which any health club of today would envy, the terraces overlooking the incredible view of the Dead Sea Valley, the princely apartments and the synagogue. However, we were there not to re-live the days of Herod but to recall the brave group of Jews who took refuge there during the war with the Romans. As we walked from place to place we could almost feel the presence of this band of Zealots.

We decided that I would do a reading from Josephus, the famous historian, who had been a witness to the events from his position with the Roman army. And so, as twilight fell, we stood in a circle while I read of the tragedy. As I read, we looked down on the ramps which the Roman leader, Flavius Silva, ordered the Tenth Legion to build so the Romans could climb the fortress and end the siege. Since the Jews were on top of Masada they had a strategic advantage and were able to hold out against the superior Roman forces by raining down rocks on the Roman soldiers as they tried to build the ramps. Flavius Silva devised a scheme. He would use Jewish prisoners to build the ramps. He gambled that the Jews would rather die than kill their own people.

Faced with the horrible choice of killing their own people or being taken and enslaved by the Romans, the Jews elected to die. Eliezer asked his people to draw lots to see who would kill the women and children and then the other men, until there would be one left who would kill himself. The instructions were clear, "There is to be food and drink left so the Romans know that we have killed ourselves not because we were starving but because we would not be slaves."

Twilight fell as I finished reading. There was silence all around and I could only think of the miracle that I, a Jewish woman after the Holocaust, should have the privilege of standing in this historic place with my child and my grandchildren. Our presence here seemed to tell the Romans, the Inquisitors, and the Nazis, that the Jews would survive.

The others must have felt the same way, for without a sound, we all turned, lit our torches and started to walk slowly down the path. I could see from my daughter's face that she shared my feeling of being part of an age-old Jewish continuity. But what of the children? How much of this had they understood?

I didn't have long to wait. As if in answer to my unspoken question, Sam turned to me and said, "Grandma." The sound of his childish voice reverberated off the walls of the ancient fortress.

"Yes darling," I said, grasping his hand more tightly. I was sure that even this small child had been touched by the drama of the moment. Every one in the group seemed to be waiting to hear what he had to say.

"Grandma," he continued, "Yesterday we saw a horse with the biggest penis in the whole world."

So much for high drama. The spell was broken and as we all finished the descent, the sounds of laughter replaced the sounds of silence.

To Celebrate in Freedom

The newspapers of December 13, 1987 said there were about four hundred thousand people on the Mall in front of the Capitol in Washington. I was one of them. We were there to pressure our government to demand that the Soviets let Jews emigrate.

There was so much excitement as we crowded together, aware of the historic significance of Jews having the confidence to make demands on governments rather than coming, hat in hand, as supplicants. It was one of the proudest days of my life. The people were impassioned but disciplined, conducting themselves with great dignity. On a political level I was thrilled to be part of the march but, more than that, on a personal level the day held very special meaning for my family and for me.

A group of us had flown down from New York together. We carried placards with the names of individual Refusniks: Furman, Sharansky, Charney, Sheba. For me they were more than names since my daughter and I had met many of them when we went to the Soviet Union to see Refusniks in 1973. Some had been prisoners then and were still being held all these many years later. Some were no longer in prison but still unable to emigrate and still others, the lucky ones, made it to freedom in Israel.

A few months before the march my daughter, Penny, her daughter, Jill, and I were discussing Jill's upcoming Bat Mitzvah.

"Grandma," Jill said, "wouldn't it be wonderful if I shared the ceremony with a Soviet twin? Mom and I think so."

I was thrilled she had made this decision. The idea of "twinning" had been developed to sensitize American Jewish children to the fact that the freedom to practice their religion, which they take so for granted, was something Jews in other lands could only dream of. The American "twin" was to write to her Soviet counterpart to share the details of her celebration of coming of age. She would write about her feelings, her portions of the Torah, even her parties and presents. She would hope the letter got through Soviet censors.

Jill was very eager to participate in the program. She had heard a great deal about the trip her mother and I had taken to the Soviet Union before she was born. So she and Penny went down to the office of the Coalition To Free Soviet Jewry and applied to be an American "twin." All the pertinent information was recorded and Jill was told that within a few days she would have the name of her twin. She could then write to her.

When the name arrived we could hardly believe it. It was Dahlia Brailovsky. Penny and I both remembered the Brailovsky family and the evening we spent in their home while we were in Moscow. Victor, the father, a talented cyberneticist, and his wife, Irina, one of the country's top mathematicians, had lost their jobs when they registered for emigration to Israel. They were reduced to giving mathematics lessons to the children of other Jews, the only people who would associate with them.

The night that we were at their home they were celebrating the end of a hunger strike which they had initiated with three other Refusnik couples to dramatize their demands to leave the country. The object of the strike was to focus international attention on the plight of Soviet Jews, in the hope that with enough of a public outcry they would be allowed to emigrate to Israel. They succeeded in getting the foreign press to cover the strike and were now waiting to see if they would be allowed to leave.

For us the whole evening was Kafkaesque. Here we sat, at a long narrow table, surrounded by fellow Jews who were having their first solid food in two weeks. The K.G.B. was walking up and down outside the apartment house and we were singing Hebrew songs and toasting each other with a L'chaim.

"Aren't you afraid" I asked, "with those thugs just outside the door?"

"What can they do to us more than they have already done? They can hurt our bodies but they can't destroy our spirit. That's what makes them crazy. We have something we really believe in and all their threats and torture won't make us give up."

Irina, still weak from the strike, was looking after her small son and serving all the delicacies they could afford. We had augmented the feast with caviar and vodka. We bought things which were unavailable to Soviet citizens, such as cans of fruit and vegetables, at the Beryoshka shops, those well-stocked stores which were only open to those with hard currency. The things we brought were such a treat for our new friends that we wished we had brought more, but they seemed pleased and anyway, after two weeks of fasting, they had to eat very carefully.

We returned home from our trip and somehow lost touch with the Brailovsky family. Now, fourteen years later our lives were to touch once again.

No answer to that gem.

"Oh my God!" I scream. "You almost rammed that car in front of us. Must you tailgate?"

The car is piloted to the side of the road and again he asks, "Would you like to drive?"

Silence for a little while and then someone else runs a red light just as he had done a few minutes before.

"Horse's ass," he fumes. "People like that should have their licenses revoked."

Should I say, "Darling, that's exactly what you just did," or should I change the subject or tune to some erudite conversation on National Public Radio? I let my non-automotive personality take over and turn on the radio. An author is being interviewed. I listen for a few minutes and then I say, "That sounds like an interesting book. Do you want to stop at the book store?"

He doesn't expect that question, so he just remains silent. All would be well except that we are now approaching our home and there are two stop signs on the way. He has a habit of speeding up before he reaches a stop sign and then jamming on the brakes. He doesn't disappoint me and, though I say nothing, my facial expression and my body language speak volumes.

We drive into the driveway, I open the garage door with the automatic opener and we each breathe a sigh of relief. We can now go into the house and resume our normal, affectionate, almost-perfect relationship.

Isn't Beauty Worth A Little Suffering?

"It's pure vanity," I say to myself. "Besides, it costs a fortune and in this world where so many are hungry, what gives me the right at seventy years of age to spend so much money to have a neck without lines?" I hear myself and, as is typical of me, I pay no attention. I do what I always do, I plan something for so far ahead that I am sure the day will never come. Then it does, as it always does, and it's too late to back out.

Now that day had come and there I was on a gurney, being wheeled into the operating room at the Manhattan Eye and Ear Hospital. I had visions of emerging with my skin so tight that I wouldn't be able to smile. I began to remember the stories well-meaning friends had told me about people they knew who had died from the anaesthetic during a similar operation, and of others who looked as if they were wearing masks. "You're so pretty," my husband, Norman told me over and over. "Why try to improve on a good thing?"

Remembering all this, I felt that I should get up off the stretcher and explain that I had changed my mind. I could tell the nurse that I made a mistake. I had done that once before but that was before the process had gone this far. Two years ago I made the decision to have my face lifted, or at least the lower part of it, which I felt was hanging down. The word around town was that, though he was the most expensive, Dr. Hogan was also the best. So Dr. Hogan it was going to be. I waited for six months to get an appointment with him. He seemed very nice and assured me that what I wanted done was simple enough. However it would be six months before he would have time to operate on me. I made the date and left the office. After all, I didn't look so awful that I couldn't wait six months.

As I walked out I bumped into someone I knew. She looked at me and at the name on the doctor's door from which I was emerging and gushed, "Oh Elaine, Dr. Hogan did your face. It's a perfect job. You'd never know that you had anything done." I figured if I looked that good I didn't need any improvements, so I went back in and canceled. To tell the truth, I was relieved.

That, as I said, was two years ago. Now things were different. I was past the point of no return. I'd had the chance to cancel and every time it crossed my mind I would look in the mirror, pull my skin skyward and resolve to go through with it. Now here I was strapped to a gurney and full of Demoral. The nurse had given me enough of it so that I couldn't change my mind if I wanted to. All I could do was lie there and feel sort of pleasantly drowsy. Did I have second thoughts? Lots of them, but I felt as if they belonged to someone else. Ideas just seemed to drift in and out of my head. I knew they were there, but they didn't seem as if they belonged to me. I couldn't keep anything straight. Everything would be all right. That Demoral is lovely stuff.

I was wheeled into what I was told was a holding room. I was groggy, but not too groggy to notice I wasn't being taken in turn. There must have been four or five other patients in the room, some, like me, on gurneys, and some in reclining brown leather chairs. One by one they were wheeled out and their places were taken by others. Only I seemed to stay where I was.

"What's going on?" I asked.

"Dr. Hogan is still working on his last case," was the answer. That caused a whole flood of worries. If he was having trouble with the last patient, maybe he'd be too tired by the time he got to me. Had he lost his touch? "Go to sleep, stupid," came my inner voice. "You asked for this."

Another, still louder voice whispered in my ear. "The doctor has only seen you twice. How the hell can he know what you want to look like? And what will you look like, some Chinese mask?"

Finally, after almost two hours, my turn came. I was wheeled into an operating room. Its large lights were shining in my eyes, and I was aware of nurses bustling about. Someone helped me from the gurney to the operating table, although I told them quite firmly that I could do it myself. Then I saw the doctor. He seemed quite fresh, not at all exhausted from the last procedure. "Please don't make me look like a seventy year old go-go dancer," I said, ever ready with the repartee. "I hear there isn't a big market for them these days."

"Just relax and go to sleep," he said in a very soothing tone. "Everything will be fine." With that, he began to draw lines on my neck and my chin. I was no longer in control. Even I could figure that out, so I decided I might as well do as I was told. I closed my eyes and the next thing I remember is being back in my room where a nurse was putting cold compresses on my eyes.

It's now a few years later. I think it was worth it. And I am comforted to know that at my age I will never do it again. Of course you can't count on it. Vanity is one of the last things to go.

Joyce

It is a Jewish custom to light a candle on the anniversary of the death of a loved one. I prefer to light it on that person's birthday. I suppose it is a matter of celebrating life and not death. There was lots to celebrate in my sister Joyce's life and so on July 20th I light my yarzhiet candle and say a prayer in her memory. As I do so I look at the picture next to the candle. In it, four women are standing in my garden, each with a smile on her face, for this was a happy occasion. It was the marriage of my son, Peter, to Barbara Wykoff. My sisters, for they are the ones in the picture, had gathered from distant places: Mickey and Joyce from Florida, Sis from Jerusalem. We were together and everything should have been wonderful but we were all aware that Joyce, the youngest, was dying of colon cancer and this would be the last family celebration we would all share.

Joyce was beautiful on this bright summer Sunday. The horrible disfigurements were still in the future, although not far off. She was wearing a pinkish-beige chiffon dress with a high neck and long sleeves. Her only ornaments, besides her smile, were a string of pearls and matching earrings. Her light brown curly hair was cut short. I treasure this picture as it is the last one ever taken of her.

I was two years old when Joyce was born and I can't remember life without her. At that time Mickey was eight and Sis was five-and-a-half. So it was almost as if we were two families. Joyce and I stuck together. Oh, I loved Mick and Sis, my grown-up sisters, and there were times when I thought Joyce was a pest, but just let anyone try to take advantage of her and I was there, defending her. And though she was half my size she did her share of defending me.

As we grew up we became closer and closer. Not only did we go to the same high school but we went to the same college as well. We shared confidences and interests, not the least of which was the U.J.A. When I became national chairman she was the obvious choice to be vice chairman in charge of training, not because she was my sister but because she was the best and had proven it in communities all over the country. She had a joie de vivre which was contagious. People loved Joyce and they loved to be with Joyce and Mike who were always ready to get involved in a party or a cause.

For a long time after she died, ten months after this picture was taken, I could only think of the last awful days, of the many times I flew to Florida to be with her. It was a terrible time. I watched her suffer and I was able to do so little to help her. Yet I learned so much from her. I learned that you don't play games with a terminally ill person. You don't say, "I know you'll get better." The most you can say is, "There's always an outside chance." When Joyce would say, "I'm terrified of dying," I could only answer, "I would be too." You must never minimize the suffering or the fear. You can only be there and listen.

A day that stands out in my memory was December 23, 1980. I was sitting on the edge of her bed while she stood in the bathroom combing her hair. Suddenly I heard a gasp.

"Oh my God!" she said. "All my hair! It's falling out!"

I ran in and there on the floor and in the brush were great clumps of hair. Joyce was sobbing.

"What will I do?" she asked over and over. "You know how afraid I am that I will end up a bald, yellow little old lady in a wheel chair. I can't let Mike see me this way. Oh God, I'm so ugly. What will I do?"

"We'll find you a wig right away," I assured her, not having the vaguest idea how to go about it. "They make wonderful ones now. You'll see, you'll get one and you'll look absolutely natural."

I looked up "Wigs" in the yellow pages and called the first number listed. The phone was answered by a harried-sounding woman. "Don't you realize this is two days before Christmas?" she snapped at me. "We can't take any new customers now. Call back in two weeks."

Quickly, before she could hang up I said, "My sister has cancer. Her hair is falling out by the handful. All her children are coming for the holidays and she can't face them this way. Couldn't you make an exception and take her?"

Her tone changed completely. "Bring her here right away. We have a special private room so she won't be embarrassed in front of the other clients."

"Come on, Joycey," I said. "Let's go. They have just what you need."

The woman was as good as her word. We were ushered into a private room and the owner of the store took care of us personally. Joyce picked out a wig that looked completely natural. The light seemed to come back into the large hazel eyes which were her dominant feature.

"Maybe when the treatments are over it will grow back again," she said with a smile. "In the meanwhile, I think I look pretty good." She did. She also bought a scarf, which had bangs sewn into the front, to wear around the house.

From that day it was downhill all the way. The chemotherapy became more difficult as her veins shrank. Her trips to the doctor were pure torture. Her hair never did grow back. Her body became swollen and distorted. Yet her spirit remained pure Joyce. "I don't want some smarmy rabbi at my funeral," she informed me as I walked into her room on one of my bi-weekly trips. "And I certainly don't want the rabbi from our synagogue. He's a real hypocrite and boy, does he emote. You and I are going to interview rabbis."

And we did. She would sit propped up on the couch while I ushered in the candidates. She finally settled on a gentle man who was liberal in his thinking and promised to soft pedal the whole issue of God.

The day came when she was too weak to walk and she was embarrassed by the way she looked, even with the wig on. Somehow I was able to persuade her to let me push her in the wheelchair to the small club in the adjacent building.

"How about a drink?" I suggested.

"What a good idea," she said. "I'd love a piña colada."

So every day she would get dressed in whatever would fit over her swollen belly, get into the chair and we would go over to the club. She would greet all her friends and proudly order a pina colada. She never took more than one sip but that drink would sit in front of her proclaiming that she was a normal woman having a cocktail with her lunch.

When she was at home she wore the scarf with the bangs instead of the wig. It was cooler and more comfortable. One evening Mike came home from the office and, after kissing her, asked, "Why do you wear that shmatta on your head?"

"I don't want you to see me bald," she answered.

He looked at her and said, "Darling, I could never see you bald." I'll always love him for that, among other things.

When I wasn't in Florida, she and I spoke on the phone at seven-thirty every morning. One day I had an eight-thirty meeting in New York and had to make an early train. I decided to call Joyce from the city after the meeting was over.

She answered the phone and said, "Elaine, I want to die but I don't want to die without you here." There were tears in her voice but she was under control.

"I'll be on the next plane," I said calmly. Then I hung up and fell apart. The people in my office were wonderful. They called the airline, got me a reservation and had someone drive me to the airport.

When I arrived she was lying in her bed, hardly able to speak, but somehow she managed to tell me that she would take no nourishment. We could wet her lips but that was all. She wouldn't even eat one of her beloved ice pops for fear that the sugar would give her a little added strength.

When her husband came home that night she said, "Mike, you promised and so did Doctor Terhune. Call him." Tears running down his cheeks, Mike did as he was told.

Soon Doctor Terhune came. He went directly into the bedroom. When he came out after what seemed a few moments he said, "You'd better go in. It won't be very long." We looked at each other, unable to speak. Then Mike got up and went into the bedroom followed by his and Joyce's sons and by me. We all stood there and looked at Joyce, the pain erased from her face, the look of suffering gone. No one questioned what had happened while the doctor was in there alone with her. It was enough she was at peace.

Joyce was fifty-four when she died, but to everyone in the family she was always "the baby". Now she was gone. My world would never be the same. I quickly called my two older sisters who were at a hotel next door and told them. They were at the apartment in a matter of minutes.

What happened next was so strange that I cannot believe it to this day. We all began to rifle through Joyce's closets and drawers with an intensity that made me think of the black-hooded women in Zorba the Greek. However we were not grabbing things for ourselves. We were packing everything in boxes to give away, as though we were trying to rid ourselves of her. We who had loved her so much.

Her brightly colored scarves went into a cardboard box along with her lace trimmed bras and panties. Her sweaters followed, then her slacks and skirts. Her shoes (she had always had such small feet) were added to the pile.

In the years that have passed I often wonder why I didn't save at least some of the handkerchiefs. I could have carried one in my purse and it would have made me feel that she with me at all times.

"You'll do my eulogy," Joyce had told me a few months before her death. Somehow I did it, but it was the hardest thing I have ever done in my life. I spoke for several minutes but all I can remember saying is "Joycey, you made a difference." And she had.

It was at least three years before I could remember the feisty pretty women Joyce had been before she got sick, before I could close my eyes and not see her swollen body and pain-filled face. Mike gave me an oil painting of her and for the longest time it hung in the back hall where I wouldn't have to confront it all the time. Finally I was able to hang it in my bedroom, look at it, and smile.

Sis, The Next To Last Visit

My older sister Doris, always called Sis, has just returned to her beautiful home in Jerusalem from Canada where she has been pronounced fine after undergoing a lung cancer operation. "Clean" is the word the doctors used. I phone her every day and instead of sounding better she tells me that she is fatigued and in great pain. Sis is not a complainer, so I feel as if I have to get there and see her.

Norm and I arrive to find her in bed, hair combed and make-up on, but too weak to get up and greet us. "Four specialists will be here in about in hour," she informs us. "They are going to decide how to treat this terrible pain in my back."

They arrive and we learn, as she does, that some microscopic bearers of pain and death have escaped the surgeon's scalpel and are beginning to grow in her spine.

Everyone faces tragedy in a different way. Sis is controlled and stoic in facing her own mortality. I want to reach out, hug her and tell her that it is all right to be frightened, that anyone in her position would be, but that isn't the way she wants the situation to be handled. She doesn't want any maudlin talk. She wants to run her household in the precise elegant way that she always has, the marble floors highly polished, the Henry Moores dusted, the silk cushions puffed and the garden pruned to perfection.

"All you Americans analyze too much," she has always told me, forgetting that she was born and brought up in New York. So what do I say to her? I lived through the same kind of thing with my sister Joyce, but Joyce was different and so was our relationship. Joyce and I shared so many values. We were equals. But to Sis, in spite of the fact that I am seventy years old and have had a fair amount of success in my life, I am still the unhousebroken kid sister with a lot of "American" hang ups. I am a feminist, of all silly things, a kind of pseudo-intellectual who butts her nose into places where she doesn't really belong, asking questions better left unasked. . . .Like, what medication the doctor is prescribing.

Sis answers with a shrug. "I won't ask him. I can't stand amateur doctors and I certainly don't intend to be one."

"You may be right, but it's your body and you're entitled to know what you put into it."

"The doctor knows what he is doing," she says. "I don't have to."

I don't press the point.

Why can't I just say, "I love you Sis and I want to be here for you."? I can't because she wouldn't want me to and so I talk about politics or her grandchildren, or mine. As she suffers the pain I sit by her bedside and pretend not to notice she's wincing.

Once, at a particularly bad moment, she says, "I never believed that there could be such agony." But she says it in an almost matter of fact voice and when the telephone rings a moment later her answer to the caller is, "Not bad, not bad at all."

She is rigid in her demands. She eats in bed but the table in the dining room must be set for us in its usual formal style. We must eat our meals on time, the main one at lunch, even though we say we would prefer to have just a sandwich.

"That's not the way we do things here," she tells us. She is big on "the way we do things." I think it makes her feel she still has control. "Norm dear," she tells my very informal husband, "one doesn't lie on the living room couch." And in her home one doesn't.

I search for topics of conversation and find that stories of our childhood are the safest. Still the silliest things can make her combative.

I say, apropos of nothing, "Isn't it strange that at my age I don't have a gray hair."

She says, "Are you trying to tell me that that's your natural color?"

"Of course not," I answer, "but my natural color is now brown and I have streaks added because I look terrible as a brunette. You know," I add, "Grandma and Mom never had any gray hair either."

"That's nonsense," she says. "Theirs was gray and so is yours. I was just noticing it this morning."

I don't argue. She is lying in bed taking morphine-based pain killers. If she says its gray, it's gray. This is no contest. This is my sister dying of cancer. I change the subject.

Then the medication seems to take effect. She gets out of bed and puts on a pretty navy-and-gold silk shirt with slacks to match. She makes up her face and combs her hair, but the effort is too much and she lies down on the bed, fully dressed. Still, it was worth the exertion. She likes the way she looks and so do we. For a moment we all feel as if she might recover.

Contents

PART III. THE REMOTE PLACES

PART IV. PROBLEMS AND ADVANTAGES FOR THE NEW-GROWTH AREAS

PART V. WHAT LIES AHEAD

Foreword

This book has two purposes. One is to describe the new population and economic growth that is taking place beyond the established suburbs of metropolitan areas and in once-remote places even farther removed from the large cities—to provide an analysis of how this growth along with other change is transforming the politics, government, and economy of America and what this is likely to mean for the future. The second is to provide a guide for those who are considering moving to this newest American frontier, whether to a place within commuting distance of some sizeable population center or farther away in one of the many self-contained communities where new opportunities abound. If such places are to be home for an increasingly larger portion of our population, as the evidence suggests, it is essential that Americans have a better understanding of where this new frontier may be leading us.

The reader will be taken on a tour of representative areas from coast to coast, a tour designed to describe the great variety of places and experiences involved and to explain why people move there, who they are, how they work and live, and the advantages and disadvantages of settling there.

There also are chapters explaining the origins of the new growth and its connection to the past. First is an overview of the dispersal of much of the population and industrial base away from old urban centers, a reversal of migration patterns that had persisted for most it was better forgotten. And in the forgetting, continuity with the past that had preceded the destruction was lost as well. He could only reconstruct what must have been.

Of those who lived here at the time of his visit, probably the majority were not born abroad. Rather, they were second-, third-, and fourth-generation Americans, many from farms and small towns, who had come because they could find jobs here. For the most part, they were never converted to urban living, much preferring the farms and towns where in the early 1900's most Americans had lived. The strong desire for independence—each family in its own domain—infected the immigrants as well. Many who prospered moved out to single-family homes. Those who remained were increasingly the old and the poor. Blacks and other minorities, many of them displaced from southern farms without skills and unprepared for urban life, moved in to claim the cheapest and oldest housing.

The sense of community that had sustained the neighborhood slipped away and the forces of destruction—neglect, despair, crime, arson for profit, the riots of the 1960's as a form of protest—took over. Block by block the neighborhood fell, structurally sound buildings along with the old decayed ones. On one corner the visitor saw a vacant apartment building of new brick and mortar marked for demolition, a symbol of the failure of successive public efforts to arrest the decay. Neither the buildings nor the families who occupied them could escape the blight.

The visitor had lived more than half a century, yet his mind could not accept the extent of abandonment in America. Spared the devastation of war for more than a century, the nation seemed bent on creating ruins of a different kind. The destruction of old hotels built to last centuries and the erection of plastic boxes out along the freeways was a relatively minor example. The draining of the working middle class from the urban centers of high density, however, was a matter of such importance, he believed, that the character of the nation was being changed in the process.

This change, like so many important shifts of history, had occurred so gradually and was so ambiguously reported that there was little understanding of what was really happening. At first, national efforts were made to save the cities in the form that had existed when he visited here four decades earlier: clusters of neighborhoods and factories around a central downtown that served as a common meeting ground for the full range of business, shopping, and entertainment activities. Those efforts, whether misguided or too small in scale, were no more successful than new buildings and subsidized social programs had been in stopping the destruction of this neighborhood.

By the late 1970's there were more reports of a great urban revival. Almost every city had impressive new downtown development—new office buildings, hotels, malls, and convention centers. A number of old neighborhoods had reasserted their sense of purpose through a multiplicity of self-help efforts. Saving and restoring old commercial and residential buildings became a national craze. The cities, however, had not really been restored. They had taken on new functions quite different from those they were created to perform.

Irrespective of political boundaries, what had been the great cities of American wealth and predominance in their regions were now subordinate nodes in vast metropolitan areas. Their function was largely to serve as centers for finance, communications, entertainment, and tourism, and as places to house minorities and other poor not assimilated into the work force. The mass of the middle class—that great proportion of the population that had sustained the cities—were simply gone, as were the factories that had saved generations of poor from dependency and despair.

There were of course exceptions: In New York and San Francisco, the new immigrants from Asia and Latin America were occupying and restoring old neighborhoods as European immigrants had done before them; in Baltimore, St. Louis, Boston, and other ethnic strongholds, the Italians or Irish, for example, maintained neighborhoods that had never been violated; and in most every city, young professionals were occupying restored housing. But for the most part the cores of the cities were now occupied by the unemployed poor, the very prosperous, and transients of various kinds. Beyond the new downtown development and restored residential streets in city after city were open spaces, abandoned factories and warehouses, and the still-decaying housing where the working middle classes once lived.

The visitor wondered where they were now, those who had abandoned, willingly or not, a form of American civilization that died very young. He had long ago lost contact with the family he had visited here. He imagined his cousin playing violin for the Tulsa Symphony, his uncle at an advanced age running a bakery in a suburban mall.

Neither they nor their descendants would want to hold a wake for the lost American city, where life was frequently difficult and work overbearing.

Yet to the visitor, the passing of the American city as it had existed during most of this century was worth noting for reasons that had little to do with preferences or economic well-being. What was important to him was that so many of the productive middle class grouped together in neighborhoods of high density and, composing a large percentage of the population, had uniquely influenced the course of American politics, government, and other institutions.

The American city had, probably more than any other force, challenged the high degree of individualism bred by small towns and rural areas. Large numbers of people living closely together felt, as scattered populations did not, the need for group cooperation and government intervention and assistance. Dense cities were the places where labor unions were most easily organized, where the national domestic programs aimed at redistributing the wealth and offering group assistance enjoyed the strongest support, where political parties could best flourish and influence national policy.

In most American cities of the past, residents had a firsthand knowledge of the economic, social, and racial groups who lived there. If there were slums or expensive homes across town, all in the city knew about them and felt their presence. A neighborhood of high crime and unemployment a few blocks from prospering ones could not be ignored. It was a threat to all. If the various groups did not mingle they brushed shoulders downtown, on the streets and on the trolleys. They felt a common destiny even though many lived in highly segregated neighborhoods. His cousin's family often talked of blacks who lived a few blocks away. They were not much tolerated on the streets near the bakery, but they went to the same schools as other groups, looked for jobs in the same factories, and shopped in the same stores. Prejudices flourished on all sides and there was violence over jobs and neighborhoods, but this was less damaging, it seemed to him, than the cold indifference or seething hatreds that had developed in the sprawling metropolitan areas. The new developments put such great distances between the economic and social groups that their knowledge of one another was limited. The negative stereotype was strengthened and there was little sense of common destiny.

The visitor walked back to the field of broken bricks where he found it advantageous to locate in the towns where the universities are and for people who want to escape the big urban areas but find most smaller places a little dull. College towns, however, with faculty and students from all over the world and with growing satellite industries that employ innovators from various regions, provide more cultural and social activities for those accustomed to city living. Former students who found those towns so confining that they could not wait to leave are among those now settling in and around college communities.

College towns are heavily represented among the scores of places that the federal government in recent years has classified as metropolitan areas, although little about them is metropolitan in character. They are of major importance to any study of the new low-density growth because even though most of them have been growing rapidly they have developed around one or more small municipalities in a way that makes them strongly resemble communities on the outer fringes of big metropolitan areas and communities in nonmetropolitan areas around small towns.

If North Carolina is a prototype for the future of America, as I believe it to be, the small metropolitan areas provide another glimpse of what America will be like over the coming decades. They are not likely to evolve into large urban or suburban places. For one, so many of them are coming along that the population projections would not support that kind of growth. But more important, the emergence of a sizeable city with suburban rings—the pattern of the past—is simply not in keeping with the kind of development that is taking place today in all regions of the nation. The big metropolitan areas—and there are scores of them—provide all the bigness that Americans can tolerate, unless, of course, a shortage of wealth and resources make a return to high density mandatory. I do not believe that will happen, at least in the foreseeable future.

I have chosen to highlight three college towns—State College, Pennsylvania; Fort Collins, Colorado; and Lafayette, Louisiana—as representative of the array of communities that in recent years have gotten themselves classified as metropolitan but in fact do not measure up to what most people think of as metropolitan—a sizeable city and its suburbs with rather extensive urban development. As many small towns have become big towns or small cities, they have brought political pressure on the government to be classified as metropolitan areas, a highly prized designation. Markets for goods and services are usually defined for advertisers and other commercial interests by metropolitan areas. In addition, metropolitan status under federal laws usually means more federal aid. As population growth has become more dispersed, the federal government has progressively retreated from its original definition established in 1950—a metropolitan area had to have a central city of at least 50,000. Now, many areas are officially classified as metropolitan that do not have a dominant central city at all. Some are composed of small towns, suburban-type sprawl, and the new low-density growth in an area inhabited by at least 100,000.

Calvin L. Beale, writing in the January 1984 issue of *American Demographics* magazine, drew up a list of functions, facilities, and conditions that might reasonably be expected to be present in a metropolitan area. They included a television station and a Sunday newspaper, airline and bus service, a four-year college, specialized hospital services, cultural activity, and a high percentage of urban development. He found one or more of these lacking in many of the areas elevated to metropolitan status since 1970.

"New York City and Jacksonville, N.C., have little in common, but they are now both official metropolitan areas," Beale wrote. "When it became metropolitan, Jacksonville had no Sunday paper, no television station, no four-year college, no museum, no local bus service, and it ranked low in the hospital facilities index. Few people seem even to have heard of Jacksonville, unless they are natives of North Carolina or served a hitch [there] in the Navy or Marines. Still, it probably is not the worst case among the new areas. Glens Falls, N.Y., appears to have the lowest score. . . . Yuba City, Calif., is not far behind."

Beale's observations point up how official statistics overstate the degree of what constitutes authentic urban development in the United States, and those contemplating moving to a small metropolitan area would do well to study his list. In 33 areas without a city of 50,000 or more that were designated as metropolitan after the 1980 census, Beale found that an average of 44 percent of the population lived in rural homes away from the towns and suburban-type sprawl. Six of the areas were more than half rural. Moreover, he noted, more than one-fourth of all metropolitan areas, which number about 330, do not contain a city of 50,000 or more people. Once, every metropolitan area did.

Most of the new areas, however, have been gaining population at a rate that exceeds the national average. And usually the growth has followed the pattern of people settling more in the outlying villages and countryside than in the towns, which have remained pretty much as they were in decades past. I chose to highlight college towns from the extensive list of small metropolitan areas because, whatever other amenities the areas may lack, most do have four-year colleges, which in almost every case was a large factor in drawing people to them. The three also reflect the general growth pattern of them all and point up the diversity that exists among them.

STATE COLLEGE, PENNSYLVANIA:
Shangri-la for a Tired Industrial State

As thousands of Penn State students and graduates can testify, State College is far from large centers of population. The town is at the geographic center of the state, 142 miles from Pittsburgh, 192 from Philadelphia, 189 from Erie, and 225 from New York. Old grads remember it taking all day to get there from almost anywhere on winding roads of the Appalachian Mountains and valleys, especially if the mode of travel was hitchhiking or a Greyhound bus. Interstate 80 between New York and Cleveland now goes within twelve miles of the town and there is commuter air service from major cities. But whatever the approach, the traveler arrives over many miles of mountains, forests, fields, and wilderness with the sense of indeed being in a remote place, a feeling that is confirmed by the fact that the new metropolitan area is often called "the happy valley," with fertile fields and woods nestled between Bald Eagle and Tussey mountains and bordered on the southeast by the Rothrock State Forest.

Penn State is big. Its campus at State College—the town acquired its name before Pennsylvania State College became a university in 1953—spreads over more than fifty city blocks and accommodates more than 30,000 students. But its bigness somehow does not overwhelm the town. College Avenue separates the two. Academia and all of its pressures and intrigues boils away in a complex of new and old buildings on the north side of the street while the relaxed commerce of a small town proceeds at its own pace across the street. The downtown gives way after a few blocks to residential areas where old houses, some built in the nineteenth century, have been restored. There are new buildings and traffic congestion, but those returning after many years away find familiar landmarks. State College is still State College.

It was the change in surrounding Centre County that was largely responsible for the area's gaining enough population to be classified as metropolitan. The Borough of State College, embracing the university, the town, and some suburbs, had a 10 percent population growth in the 1970's, to 36,130 people. But the remainder of Centre County grew at the rate of 15 percent, to 76,630. Overall, the county had had 112,760 people, or 12,760 more than needed for it to qualify as metropolitan. Under the federal government's loose definition of what constitutes an urban place—every town of 2,500 qualifies—54 percent of the area's population was urban and 46 percent rural. Most of the growth was in scattered townships and boroughs, in rural subdivisions, and along roads and highways. For Pennsylvania, which had been losing much of its population to the West and South, the growth was extraordinary. The area's growth slowed in the deep recession of the early 1980's, when state colleges were on austerity budgets, but was expected to continue through the decade.

The attractions of Centre County as a place to live are readily apparent. There are numerous lakes, trout streams, ski slopes, golf courses, hiking trails, campgrounds, and caves to explore. The area has five airports and a glider port for ridge soaring. There are art and historic museums, theater, and ballet on Nittany Mountain. "There's culture, there's sports, there's everything whether it's stamps, African violets, or the violin," said Bill Welch, executive editor of the *Centre Daily Times*. Small industries feed off the university—a manufacturer of weather instruments, for example, attracted by the university's meteorology school.

There are small, innovative businesses scattered through the county, such as a roadside stand selling only wine from vineyards developed with help from the university's agricultural division and small craft and specialty shops. The county has sophisticated planning and zoning not usually found in small metropolitan areas. Officials of the Centre Regional Council of Governments say that in the future commercial and industrial growth will be tightly controlled to ensure the kind of quality economic base the community wants.

Some might find Centre County a little too precious, like areas of Vermont with pastel houses and fat cows neatly pasted on green hills. The population is 98 percent white. Few blacks, Hispanics, or foreign-born have found their way to Centre County, at least not to take up permanent residence. Yet the county lacks the homogenization of the kind found in large-city suburbs, where incomes, interests, age, and class tend to be much the same. The newcomers looking for the amenities that the county has to offer merge with the native population of farmers, merchants, and blue-collar workers. As a result there is a mix at the shopping centers and other public places of people of high and low incomes, of intellectuals with ninth-grade dropouts, of those who like ballet with those who prefer country music, of pickup trucks with Volvos. Those differences are of little concern in places of such low density—105 acres of land for every man, woman, and child in the new metropolitan area of State College.

FORT COLLINS, COLORADO:
The Baby Boomers Take Over

While State College remains serene and somewhat remote, Fort Collins, which also offers majestic scenery and outdoor recreation, is on the fast track of the development and population growth that is taking place in an unbroken strip of metropolitan areas from Pueblo north through Colorado Springs, Denver, and Boulder to the Wyoming border, a distance of more than two hundred miles. Fort Collins, in fact, offers a picture of what life may be like in the future for many millions of Americans who now live in more traditional places, if current trends continue as expected. This metropolitan area of 150,000 is growing so fast that it could eventually turn into another mountain city like Denver with skyscrapers, congestion, and smog, but that is not considered likely. The new pattern of scattered growth with easy access to mountain lakes and ski slopes is too well-established. In any in the central cities and commuted into the suburbs. Now, almost a decade later, the figures are believed to be weighted even more to those who both live and work in the suburbs or their fringes. In a section of the study entitled "Policy Implications," Fulton pointed out that, "It has long been a fundamental assumption of planners that mass transit would provide the ultimate remedy to the urban transportation problem by reshaping urban form and by modifying consumer behavior." In other words, the availability of mass transit did not keep people in the city, nor did it keep the suburbs compact. As long as automobiles are available and affordable, the availability of public transportation is not a strong enough force to persuade people to live where the planners think they should. "Given the low-density dispersion of residences and work places," Fulton continued, "policy makers need to maintain realistic expectations of what public transportation can accomplish. . . . Public transportation policies should be formulated in coordination with and in anticipation of demographic trends instead of depending on the alteration of such trends in order to achieve such success."

The study, however, did not suggest how a public transportation system could be designed so that it would work at reasonable cost for either the old-style suburbs or, especially, for the new low-density development. It pointed out that the Minneapolis–St. Paul area had been almost alone in increasing the use of public transportation in the suburbs by an aggressive program of adding express buses and special vehicles for the elderly and handicapped and in maintaining low fares. The subsidies required for such a system, however, increased markedly over the ten-year period, a public cost that citizens of most areas refuse to bear, especially those in the fringe areas where low taxes, minimum public services, and individual initiative usually are given even higher precedent than in the older suburbs. Metropolitan areas in the West increased their use of public transit in the suburbs and beyond, but the study showed that the population had increased at an even greater rate, for a net loss in public transit use.

No one has come up with a public transportation system that would serve many people in the growing areas of low density other than rail or bus commuter lines that people can feed into with their cars or trucks: the park and ride concept. These, however, are usually to take workers out of their immediate area into the suburban ring or downtown, not to the increasing number of jobs or shopping centers nearer their homes. Indeed, public transit is rarely considered in low-density areas until traffic jams become burdensome, which is not unusual. Northern Louisiana is not a place where one would expect major traffic tie-ups. But Interstate 20 between Shreveport and Monroe, a distance of a hundred miles, is filling up so fast with long-distance commuters living in the country that F. Lester Martin, a professor of architecture at Louisiana Tech University and a member of a citizens' committee set up to study the problem, said, "We're heading for a collision of too many cars. We have to find some alternative method of transportation." The only answer, his committee concluded, was the park and ride concept, which would provide more bus, van, or rail service along the same interstate highway. "The automobile will be with us forever," Martin concluded. "Americans are accustomed to getting out of their car and going to their own door."

THE REMOTE PLACES

Part III

music" was recently in vogue, but not "hard country," which is about prisons and unrequited love. "It's a format that probably would not go anywhere else," disc jockey Tom Healy said in 1980 when the changed character of the place first became apparent. Old New England houses with barn and drying room attached were much in demand. The new population has made New Hampshire a puzzle of statistics. One of the most rural states, it has fewer farmers per capita than all but one other state, but it is the fourth most industrialized state, with the highest percentage of employees in high-tech industry. Its population grew by 25 percent in the 1970's and the Census Bureau predicted it will grow another 48 percent by the year 2000, to 1.35 million.

When the factories and people began descending on New Hampshire, political leaders and journalists speculated that the new growth could change the political character of the state, which has long been a stronghold of old-fashioned Republican conservatism. Many of the new arrivals were from Boston, then a bastion of liberalism. Many prided themselves on being political independents. Most predictions about how they might change the state were that they would be more in the mainstream of American politics and in the state's presidential primaries would make it harder for conservatives such as Ronald Reagan to win.

Both the 1980 and the 1984 primaries proved the predictions wrong. Reagan won over George Bush, then cast as a moderate, in the 1980 Republican primary, with strong support from the newcomers. And Walter Mondale lost to Senator Gary Hart of Colorado, cast as the more conservative of the two, in the 1984 Democratic primary. Reagan had no opposition in 1984, yet when *New York Times* reporter Fox Butterfield took a class of Syracuse University journalism students to a shopping center in the new-growth area to interview voters, they had trouble finding anyone who intended to vote in the Democratic contest. "They were all for Reagan on the Republican side," Butterfield said. The new New Hampshire turned out to be a stronghold of the new conservatism rather than the old, with both blue-collar and professional young people making up a strong segment of the electorate, just as they do in most areas of new low-density growth. As in North Carolina, they were not so much embracing all that the Reagan candidacy stood for as they were rejecting Democratic politics of the past.

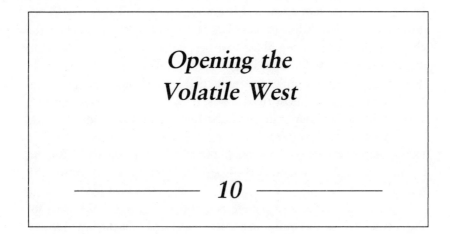

Opening the
Volatile West

---------- 10 ----------

Early maps of the United States depicted the West as the Great American Desert, and by comparison to the rest of the nation it still is. The West, constituting more than half of the nation's land area, receives less than 15 percent of the total precipitation that falls on the entire country, and great portions of it are too mountainous or too far from water sources to be habitable. Yet in the 1970's it was the fastest-growing region in the nation, particularly the mountain states, whose population increased by 37 percent and is continuing at a rapid rate in the 1980's.

Western population shifts also are the most volatile. As Governor Richard D. Lamm of Colorado pointed out, the mountain West historically is a land of boom and bust. Of the 63 counties in his state, 31 had more people in 1900 than in 1970, when the current boom was getting under way. "We have had it all happen before," he said. "They came to get the gold, the silver, the lead, the zinc, the molybdenum." They left the region marred by ghost towns. In the 1970's newcomers were back, building new towns in new places in search of coal, shale, and uranium. Through the 1970's some communities grew so fast they could not provide the infrastructure needed for public services. "We have an influx of new businesses and people seeking new styles of life," Lamm said. By the mid-1980's the growth showed no sign of stopping, even though many of the small mining and manufacturing towns were once again drying up and despite warnings that the supply of impounded water which sustained the growth could not last forever.

Western authorities are quick to point out, however, that the new growth has a broader base than in the past. A study conducted by the Los Alamos Scientific Laboratory in 1980 showed that manufacturing, retirement, and recreation had a stronger effect on migration into outlying areas of the mountain West than ever before. Booms of the past were heavily dependent on mining and other economic incentives. Recently, however, the mountain West, more than any other region, has attracted people seeking an independent lifestyle in scenic open spaces far removed from the cities and big suburbs. Unless the region runs out of water, which does not seem likely in the places where people are settling, it is reasonable to expect the high rate of growth to continue. This can be demonstrated in innumerable communities. I have chosen two, one in northern Idaho, the other in western Arizona.

On Lake Pend Oreille near the town of Sandpoint, Idaho, the houses hidden by evergreens that cover the steep slopes look like alpine vacation homes with multiple levels and large decks reaching out toward the water. They are in fact year-round homes for working couples with children. One August afternoon, when the children were off somewhere in the woods, Diane Hudson sat on the deck sipping white wine and explaining how she, her husband, and two grade-school children came to move from San Francisco to this land of mountains and lakes, to where Idaho narrows just before it joins the Canadian border. The Hudsons were young professionals who had taken salary cuts in order to live in Idaho. "Both of us had been married before," she said. "One reason for my divorce from my first husband was disagreement over where we would live. I wanted to come here for the children. The change has been good for them. It's not just the bad influences back there. Here they are independent. There is no need for organized play. They find their own entertainment, and we do not worry about where they are. They learn to think for themselves."

In the 1970's much of the mountain West, including parts of rural California, became the latest refuge not only for people moving from the East but for those who found the cities and suburbs on the West

Coast, the landing point for restless migrants over several decades, less of a promised land than many had thought. The area around Sandpoint and Coeur d'Alene attracted many from Los Angeles, Fresno, San Francisco, and Sacramento. More than half of the Coeur d'Alene's police force came from the Los Angeles police department. "Many of those from California cities bought houses in the 1960's for, say, $40,000, which they sold recently for $100,000 to $150,000," said a planning officer for Kootenai County, which surrounds the small city of Coeur d'Alene. "They put that equity into land and a house here which, despite inflation, still go for less than those in California. They can do this, make less money, and still live as well or better than they did back there."

As in every region, most of the growth was not in town but in outlying areas, a pervasive trend based on both economics and the desire by many Americans to escape urban settings. The new growth was in rural subdivisions or on five- to ten-acre plots along the rivers and lakes and on the mountainsides. Many of the new settlers were living a marginal existence best suited for the country. "We have a lot of mobile homes," said Joseph A. Scorcio of the Kootenai County planning and zoning commission. "There's a saying that what you see is a five-acre farm, a pickup truck, a mobile home, and a starving horse. And that's all there is."

(Mobile homes have been a prime facilitator of the new scattered growth, especially in the West. In December 1984 the Census Bureau issued a special report that in 1980 10.2 million Americans lived in mobile homes. There were 3.9 million units, not counting another .8 million not lived in full-time. Most were outside metropolitan areas and two-thirds were built between 1970 and 1980, when the new scattered growth was most rapid. Nationally, mobile homes constituted 5.3 percent of the housing stock, but that percentage was much higher in the mountain West—18 percent in Wyoming; 13 percent in Arizona, Montana, Nevada, and New Mexico; 12 percent in Idaho. In most of the Northeast, the use of mobile homes is minimal, constituting less than 1 percent of the housing stock in Connecticut, New Jersey, Massachusetts, and Rhode Island, in part because of zoning laws against them. They have become popular because they are much cheaper than conventional housing and in some areas have provided the only means of retaining single-family housing. Many Americans distance that barges had to travel, so many billions had been spent in prior decades it was too late to stop.

The other factor favoring savings in construction was that the states were no longer engaged in building colleges and other institutions, with the exception of prisons, at the fast rate they were in the decades after World War II. Most states in the 1980's were committed to spending a larger share of their capital budgets for maintenance and repairs than they had in the past. Yet in the face of continued demand for new facilities and widespread opposition to higher taxes, no one really knew whether the nation, and its political system, was capable of assuring that repairs could keep pace with deterioration at the same time it was forced to spend billions cleaning up toxic wastes and diverting resources to other uses such as the military buildup and paying interest on the staggering national debt.

The issue barely mentioned in the infrastructure debates but of paramount importance is that which bears directly on the new scattered development: Can the nation maintain its old facilities while continuing to build anew at a rate greater than the growth of the population? There are two major aspects to this question. One is the trend toward putting more and more space between people—fewer occupants per housing unit, fewer housing units per acre, greater distances between developed areas—so that much more investment and maintenance is required per person than in the past. The other is the practice of building new facilities and abandoning or underusing the old as the population continues to move outward from the central cities and settle in new, undeveloped places.

This practice can be seen clearly in the single category of public schools. In almost every major metropolitan area it is possible to find an invisible arc or circle, one that is moving slowly outward toward the metropolitan fringe. On one side of the line, the communities are closing public schools, many of them built only a few years ago, and selling or leasing them for uses for which they were never intended. On the other side of the line, the school boards frequently have trouble keeping up with the demand for new classrooms. There the scene is frequently reminiscent of the suburbs almost everywhere during the post–World War II baby boom, with some schools using portable classrooms or conducting school by shifts.

On Long Island, where suburban development has been marching eastward from New York City for several decades, the invisible line has moved through all of Nassau and much of Suffolk counties, which together make up a suburban conglomerate of 2.6 million people with no central city. The Syosset Central School District in Nassau, for example, built sixteen schools between 1954 and 1963, but enrollment declined from 8,600 in 1971 to 6,400 in 1980. Young couples with children found housing there too expensive and moved to developments farther out. Over a period of several years, school officials had to make difficult decisions of which schools to close and which to keep open, invariably causing controversy among patrons.

Disposing of the closed schools was almost as difficult. The East Meadow District, also in Nassau, was finally converted into seventy-eight apartments for the elderly after it had failed as a dinner theater, dance studio, and center for social causes. In many instances, on Long Island and elsewhere, the schools were torn down and the land put to other uses. In a suburb north of Chicago, Niles East High School, built to accommodate 2,500 students and still structurally sound, was closed in 1981 because of a shortage of students while thirty miles farther north, in Prairie View, residents were voting on a bond issue to build a new high school because of an influx of students. Even in fast-growing states, the process was the same. In Utah, where overall school enrollment was increasing by 3,000 a year, Salt Lake City closed twenty-two schools over a period of several years, while outlying school districts could not keep up with the demand for classrooms.

Building and abandoning schools was, of course, only one of the more noticeable aspects of a bigger process. The same was true to a lesser degree of hospitals, firehouses, police stations, jails, shopping centers, churches, synagogues, hotels, and other public and private buildings. Basically it was a process of development taking place considerably faster than both the overall growth in population and the rate at which facilities wear out or become obsolete.

The Carter administration in its closing months took two actions that were related to this. It issued a policy that said, in effect, federal funds could not be used in some instances where there was an unneeded duplication of facilities; a specific example was the construction of a shopping center outside a town or city that was willing and able to preserve its downtown shopping district. Carter was voted

Opportunities and Challenge for the Twenty-first Century

15

It should be obvious to all by now that even though Americans are unpredictable in many ways, a pattern of growth is under way that has not yet run its course. The spread of the population into new areas of low density is clearly not the passing fad that some believed it to be. Rather, it is an alternative to both the big cities and their massive suburbs, one that a sizeable number of people have chosen. And nothing on the horizon strongly indicates an end to the trend. If that is so, then Americans, despite failures of the past and all of the problems facing the new kind of growth, have an opportunity to build more livable communities than were created in either the cities or the suburbs—ones that would foster diversity, not large concentrations of sameness; continuity with the past, not obliteration of old landmarks that remind us what we were in generations past; a blending of development with nature beyond what the suburbs or urban parks provided, not the seemingly endless dominance of concrete and buildings that the automobile culture has imposed on most of our urban-suburban landscape.

Before discussing how that opportunity might be seized, or once again allowed to pass us by, it is appropriate to examine why the trend is likely to continue. There are several important aspects to this.

In one sense, the new growth is a product of affluence, of people's ability to live where they wish. An example of how crucial this is can be seen in population projections for Florida in the 1950's. Predictions of the state's future growth were woefully understated. It was not anticipated that so many millions of elderly would have the means to settle there in retirement, that laid-off automobile workers in Detroit would have enough unemployment compensation to winter in the Florida sun, or that college students in virtually every state could find their way to southern beaches for spring break. Nor was it expected elsewhere that ski resorts, tennis camps, and all manner of water holes would provide the economic base for new communities that had never been populated before. In the 1950's few Americans could afford to commute long distance in their own cars, even if expressways had existed to carry them. The list goes on of new low-density growth occurring because people for the first time had the economic means of living in ways that suited them rather than being confined by the reality of marginal incomes and savings.

If prosperity for any large sector of the population continues, even at a lower level than in the past, then it is reasonable to expect the new growth to continue with it. The results of a Gallup poll taken in February 1985 asking people where they preferred to live were consistent with others taken during the past fifty years. "Given the opportunity," George Gallup, Jr., concluded from the findings, "almost half of American adults would move to towns with fewer than 10,000 inhabitants or to rural areas." The national sample of 1,557 persons were asked, "If you could live anywhere you wished, which one of these places would you prefer?" The responses were as follows:

Large city (1 million or more population)	7%
Medium city (100,000 to 1 million)	15%
Small city (50,000 to 100,000)	16%
Large town (10,000 to 50,000)	13%
Small town (2,500 to 10,000)	23%
Rural area, on a farm	17%
Rural area, not on a farm	8%
Don't know	1%

The 38 percent who said they would like to live in a large, medium, or small city were then asked, "Where in the city—within the city itself, or in the suburbs outside the city?" Of those who preferred a large city, 64 percent wanted to live inside the city boundaries, but a preference for the suburbs was much stronger in the other two categories, with 66 percent preferring the suburbs of the medium-sized city and 74 percent of the small city. Overall, the poll showed that the vast majority of Americans simply do not like large cities and there is no ground swell, either, for the large suburbs.

If Americans had moved to where planners and government officials in the 1950's and 1960's thought they would and should, they would have settled in compact new cities: in new, more dense forms of suburban development and in revitalized and restored old city neighborhoods. Yet there has been a minimum of that. Instead, people have spread out in virtually every imaginable way.

A deep and prolonged depression, which some economists say is not out of the question, could slow the process, or halt it temporarily. The 1982 recession caused a slowing of people moving from one region or state to another. With unemployment high, families doubled up with one another in whatever housing units were available or could be afforded. Population growth slowed or stopped in areas where it had occurred at a rapid rate for several years. But once the recovery came, growth and development resumed under the same patterns as before.

In some ways, however, declining income, once people see they are not likely to do much better, actually fosters new low-density growth. If we continue to see high wage industries replaced by low wage ones and by services—the $12-an-hour automobile worker, for example, having to settle for minimum wage in a fast-food outlet—then the North Carolina model becomes even more relevant. Low-density development patterns evolved there, in part, as a result of skimpy wages—those in textiles, apparel, and furniture. A minimal income can increase the attractiveness of cheaper land and housing, of part-time farming or vegetable gardening. Nor does the possibility of further energy shortages pose a severe threat to the new growth. During the late 1970's there were predictions that the rapid increase in gasoline prices would result in a return to the cities. This, however, did not happen to any significant degree. What was forgotten was that jobs, like people, have been scattered over wide areas, and to reach the workplace from exurban areas frequently requires no more, sometimes less, time and use of energy than reaching them from urban settings. Moving people within access of mass transit, even when they are willing to go, is at best of marginal help in saving energy, simply because housing patterns do not generally facilitate its use.

Changes in technology and the economy that facilitated the spread of the population in the first place, and that are expected to continue, also are likely to favor more growth of low-density communities. As use of computers and sophisticated communications systems increases, more and more people will be able to live anywhere. Industry and commerce has shown no general tendency to return to centralization of its operations within urban centers. United States Steel Corporation, for example, in its efforts to modernize its production, has announced it would build smaller plants at scattered locations across the country. Pittsburgh, the once-mighty steel center, has been diversifying its economy in the sure realization that it will never again be as dependent on heavy industry. Across the nation, industrial and office parks are still going up beyond the beltways around the cities, opening new job opportunities for people in outlying communities. Three major new automobile factories were announced for rural areas at mid-decade—Toyota in northern Kentucky and General Motors in central Tennessee and Illinois.

Some changes that have occurred since 1980, however, have stirred some speculation that the spread of the population away from urban centers may be over, with migration patterns returning to the earlier norm of urbanization. Population estimates in the first half of the decade indeed showed that nonmetropolitan areas were no longer growing faster, but slower, than metropolitan ones. More housing construction was occurring in metropolitan areas. Many remote small communities, especially in the South, were experiencing plant closures because of foreign imports. New high-tech industry that virtually every community wanted was established mostly in metropolitan areas to be close to related industries and urban amenities. Not as many people were striking out to live in rural areas with rustic lifestyles.

To conclude from this, however, that the nation was returning to the pattern that had been dominant in the twentieth century—that of mass migration to urban centers—was, as John D. Kasarda of the University of North Carolina pointed out, to misunderstand what the scattered new growth was all about. "Deconcentration is continuing," he said.

First, definitions were inadequate. Many areas that had been classified as nonmetropolitan in the 1970's had been reclassified as metropolitan in the 1980's, even though they had not undergone much if any change in character. Metropolitan areas now cover 560,880 square miles, roughly a fifth of the total land area of the forty-eight contiguous states. Within the metropolitan areas, only 52,017 square miles, or less than 10 percent of the total amount of land, are urbanized under federal definitions. "Metropolitan areas" thus cover vast expanses of thinly populated land and wilderness. They include much of the Appalachian Trail, deserts of southern California and Arizona, about half of Florida and California, most of the Northeast and Middle West from Massachusetts to Illinois, and a sizeable portion of the rest of the states except those in the Great Plains and mountain West.

Population estimates at mid-decade showed that the shift from the northern states to the South and West was continuing, that between 1980 and 1985 the nation had gained about 11 million residents, with half the gain occurring in the states of Texas, California, and Florida and the other half largely in the mountain West, the Southwest, and the South Atlantic states. Thus the population growth was largely in states where low-density development is generally pronounced. And within the metropolitan areas of all regions, the fastest growth was in exurban places, whether around Boston, New York, Baltimore, Washington, Atlanta, Chicago, Kansas City, Dallas, Houston, Denver, Seattle, or San Francisco. Some old industrial cities such as New York and Chicago had stabilized after severe losses in the 1970's while others such as Cleveland, Detroit, St. Louis, and Baltimore were continuing to lose, though at a slower rate than in the previous decade. The rich farmlands in the Middle West and South were declining at an even greater rate than in the past, owing to the prolonged depression of the agricultural economy. But the farm belt, as pointed out earlier, had never been a part of the new growth except in atypical places.

New metropolitan areas, small state capitals, the fringes of large metropolitan areas, the Ozark Mountains, the western settlements, the coastal and lake areas, the mountains of eastern Kentucky, southern New Hampshire, and others—all were still growing in 1985, most at a rate greater than the national average. All those places, and more, have established an economic and population base that promises continued growth, not retrenchment.

Probably of even more significance for future growth, however, is that in all populated areas of the United States the transition from the traditional patterns—unified city-suburbs, small-town and rural environs—to one of dispersed communities everywhere has been completed. By dispersed communities, I mean the nodal concept in which different parts of a broad area serve different functions and people move from one to the other without regard to old boundaries. Suburbanites go to the central city for certain purposes such as entertainment. They live in one suburb but work, shop, visit friends, and go to restaurants in others, often miles away. The sense of place, both psychologically and realistically, has broadened. People think of Manhattan as a rare, self-contained community, but it is self-contained only for the poor. The middle class makes a great exodus on weekends and summer months to the suburbs, beaches, and country places in numbers unprecedented in the past, an escape many consider as essential to their lives as the amenities found a few blocks away. People in and around small towns routinely travel over wide areas for services and entertainment that formerly were grouped on the town square. As a result, whether in the country or the city, the dispersed community extends over a morass of town, city, county, and other political jurisdictions established under the old order, a fact that underscores the enormity of the change.

The dispersed community, now virtually universal, does not encourage a return to high-density development. There is no longer any all-purpose center to attract it. The transition to the new order was made complete when it became apparent during the 1970's that the old high-density cities would not be restored as all-purpose centers but that each would become instead another node within a wider community. There has long been enough land for filling in the suburbs and thinned-out central cities with high-rise apartments and town houses. But it has not occurred to an extent that would begin to match the spread of development in new areas. Americans want space, not density.

This does not mean that the new low-density communities will eventually replace the old cities and the more dense suburbs. Many people prefer living there. The vertical city with shocks of high-rises, shocks of people, and all the diversity and excitement that it breeds has wide appeal, at least as a place to visit. Cities like New York and Los Angeles are not likely to be surpassed as places to assimilate foreign-born. Many of the suburbs condemned for their blandness have developed character and become more diverse as they have aged. It is simply that all indicators point to the new places of low density and those yet to be developed as areas of fastest growth.

More is involved in this than affluence, technology, and preferences by most Americans for smaller places to live. We have done very badly on the whole with both cities and suburbs, so badly that it is not surprising so many have been looking for an alternative. As early as the 1960's, there were predictions that the old industrial cities were obsolete. Eugene Raskin, professor of architecture at Columbia University, wrote in 1969 that the big cities were dinosaurs doomed to extinction in the form they took at the time. "We are shifting, not so slowly, to a pattern of existence that is independent of cities, that gets along just fine without cities, and to a way of life whose members, a generation or two from now, will look back upon the urban period of man's history with perhaps some romantic fondness, but certainly more than a tinge of horror." He then went on, in a little book entitled *Sequel to Cities*, to describe pretty much what has happened since.

Cities had become enlarged because they alone could provide what industries needed in access to markets and supply and in infrastructure. They produced "horror" when they became impacted with poor minorities seeking jobs at the very time the old industries became obsolete or began moving out under a new order of technology, communications, and transportation. Some of the old cities will survive with a substantial portion of their current population numbers intact by taking advantage of their new role in finance, information processing, and tourist centers—New York being the prime example. There is now talk of "wiring" the old cities to provide easy access to computer and other information systems, thus providing another kind of infrastructure than that which appealed to the old industry. Even so, as we can see already in New York, the "dual city"—made up of the wealthy and the poor—cannot accommodate the full range of classes, races, and incomes as it did under the old industrial economy. For one thing, there are virtually no entry-level jobs for poor minorities with minimum skills.

Yet in building the suburbs as an alternative to the cities, the result in many instances was almost as unfortunate as the rapid decline of what had been left behind. It is still impossible for many people to even drive through the tiers of large suburbs around big cities without

becoming offended at what has happened, although time has blurred
the offense in the same way a prisoner becomes accustomed to his
cell. It is not so much the endless pavement and vast stretches of
vehicles spouting noxious fumes, or the repeated sight of fast-food
outlets, shopping centers, and bland commercial buildings stamped
out of the same mold that become offensive by constant repetition.
What is most disturbing are the enclaves, one compound after the
other of people of like incomes, race, occupations, and interests bunched
together in large numbers—even in municipalities of 50,000 or more—
insulated from the diversity of life that every man, woman, and child
of previous generations experienced to some extent.

The cities were victims of forces beyond their control. Always open
to the uneducated and unwashed, they were overcome by economic
and political changes that left them with an unprecedented social
burden too large to bear without the kind of upheavals we have seen.
Most of the suburbs were deliberately created to provide barriers to
the unassimilated. The manner and purpose for which they were built
was a radical departure from the nation's traditions. In the past, of
course, some towns would not have blacks or Indians there after
sundown, but their exclusivity was not a general condition. Nor did
confining people of different class and race to certain neighborhoods
constitute either the kind or scale of exclusivity we have now, because
the excluded under the former patterns of development were nevertheless an integral part of the community, to be seen and dealt with
in one way or another by all.

The experience of fair housing enforcement is old enough now to
render a judgment. The laws have been on the books and a part of
government policy now for two decades. Yet it is hard to find any
other law sanctioned by Supreme Court rulings so flagrantly violated
and ignored. Middle-class blacks, also anxious to escape the cities,
have begun to move into white suburbs, and opposition to their doing
so is diminishing. For poor blacks, however, the record is consistent.
White middle-class communities, with rare exceptions, simply will
not tolerate them. George Romney, when he was Secretary of Housing
and Urban Development in the Nixon administration, sought to scat-
ter low-income housing through the metropolitan areas in a way that
no one community would be overburdened by a poverty population
but that chronically unemployed would be near jobs opening in the

suburbs. His plans were soon squelched, however, both by the Nixon White House and the suburban communities he sought to integrate. No administration since has made any serious attempt to open the suburbs to poor minorities. Local efforts, where they have been attempted, have met with no more success despite court rulings to support them. At the same time, some black leaders also have discouraged integration moves on grounds that black political power would be diluted in the process. In the meantime, concentrations of poor minorities in the central cities have increased as entry-level jobs have moved steadily farther away. The chronic condition of unemployment, welfare dependency, broken families, poverty, and crime has been passed from generation to generation and no one has been able to find a solution. Most social scientists ascribe to the view of Richard P. Nathan of Princeton University that this continuing failure of the nation to assimilate the urban poor is "the most critical problem facing America."

Yet it is one that in the last few years has received progressively less attention by news organizations and by government bodies. As the middle class has continued to move farther away from the core of the older cities, there is less talk of the "white noose" around cities or of "festering ghettos." Much of the society has come to accept the condition of the urban poor as one that cannot be helped by government policies and programs. As a result, some commentators refer to the old urban areas as "hidden cities."

There is little evidence, then, that the middle class consciously dislikes the suburbs because of their exclusivity. On the other hand, there is evidence that a large proportion of Americans have never felt comfortable with the structure of the modern metropolitan area, with masses of poor concentrated in their enclaves and the remainder of the population in theirs according to incomes and class. They are no more comfortable with this than they are with vast settlements that have no common center, a mockery of both town and city, or with the great stretches of ugly development that everyone has to drive through and endure. And this discomfort seems to be a major reason so many have been seeking an alternative.

At the same time, however, we face the seemingly ambiguous reality that during the latter part of the twentieth century, as the population has shifted away from the cities, Americans have become more urbane,

more appreciative of amenities found largely in the cities, more in-
clined to crowd art galleries, to attend legitimate theater, to frequent
restaurants that thrive best in urban settings, to favor old restored
buildings, to seek out shops and markets with an international flavor,
to enjoy the stimulating environment that only real cities can provide.
This being true, it would appear that much would depend in the
future on the choice that people make, whether to give up one form
of lifestyle for another, to forgo an urban environment with its various
advantages for a seemingly duller, though more independent and eco-
nomical, existence in the new areas of low density.

In truth, however, only a small percentage of the population can
elect to have a secure urban environment in a large city, one in which
they feel comfortable in most respects. That choice is open only to
those with a comparatively high income, certainly no more than 5 to
10 percent of the people. New York City, with its great variety of
urban and cultural attractions, provides the extreme example. New
York is depicted in the press as a city of throbbing vitality and prosperity, and for many it is; but not for the great middle class of marginal
incomes that once inhabited its boroughs and enjoyed its amenities
of affordable housing; safe streets, parks, and subways; educational
and cultural offerings available to everyone. Not anymore. The family
with, say, $500 a month to spend on rent has no real choice between
electing to stay in the city and settling on the New Jersey meadows.
This choice is reinforced by recent economic development and housing
construction that have been pushing outward ahead of population
movements. In other words, the developers, providing comparatively
low-cost shelter for both families and industries, are creating a low-
density, exurban environment that a large segment of the population
is more than willing to occupy.

Another point about the attraction of urban amenities is crucial to
where people who have a choice elect to live. Those with means who
live in outlying areas are highly mobile. They are rarely confined to
their immediate environment. When they do not travel on their own,
as many do both in this country and abroad, they regularly attend
conventions, at employer expense, that have increasingly become a
standard part of our modern culture. A five-day stay in New York,
New Orleans, San Francisco, or other popular convention centers
once or twice a year is usually enough to satiate their craving for

urban life, especially when urban amenities are regularly transported into their homes by way of television or into their shopping centers with a well-stocked wine and cheese store, a New York–style deli, or often a porn shop. Rarely do you encounter a citizen of the new low-density areas who is not familiar with the streets, sights, sounds, and smells of a downtown Chicago, Philadelphia, or Boston. If we have become a nation of people without strong roots in any particular community, as I believe we have, we also are a people who now draw our sustenance from a range of environments that together have wiped out the former distinctions between city and town, urban and rural, suburban and exurban.

The areas of new growth beyond the cities and large suburbs may well be the last remaining settlements not dependent on agriculture where change is more than marginally practicable and where communities can be fashioned that are in keeping with the historic American tradition of fairness and openness, where the scale of development is reduced in a way that each community can be whole in itself, not a one-dimensional segment of a galaxy. This was the idea behind the drive a decade ago for new cities, where there would be jobs and housing for all income groups living in close proximity. New self-contained cities were a plan that was rejected, in part because it is not real cities that most Americans want, it is space, and that makes all the difference.

In the first place, the new development is being imposed on a native population that usually is quite diverse, especially in the South and areas of the Southwest where minorities are on the land and in small towns. Unlike the suburbs, there is space enough for those people to remain rather than to be driven out by development, as was done by growth of the big suburbs. With rare exceptions, all of the little towns and residential roads in their path were either destroyed or changed so drastically they cannot be recognized today for what they were. The new growth, for the most part, is taking place over so wide an area and is so far removed from large cities that the old settlements usually remain amid the new.

The new settlers in low-density areas tend to be mostly white, skilled, and conservative in the sense of not liking government regulation and interference. Nevertheless, it is not likely that those communities would offer the kind of solid line of resistance to poor people